Unsaid

Unsaid

ANALYZING HARMFUL SILENCES

Lois Presser

⊞

UNIVERSITY OF CALIFORNIA PRESS

University of California Press
Oakland, California

© 2023 by Lois Presser

Library of Congress Cataloging-in-Publication Data

Names: Presser, Lois, author.
Title: Unsaid : analyzing harmful silences / Lois Presser.
Description: Oakland, California : University of California Press,
  [2023] | Includes bibliographical references and index.
Identifiers: LCCN 2022022491 (print) | LCCN 2022022492 (ebook) |
  ISBN 9780520384934 (cloth) | ISBN 9780520384941 (paperback) |
  ISBN 9780520384958 (ebook)
Subjects: LCSH: Silence—Sociological aspects. | Power (Social sciences)
Classification: LCC BJ1499.S5 P74 2023 (print) | LCC BJ1499.S5 (ebook) |
  DDC 302.2—dc23/eng/20220727
LC record available at https://lccn.loc.gov/2022022491
LC ebook record available at https://lccn.loc.gov/2022022492

32 31 30 29 28 27 26 25 24 23
10 9 8 7 6 5 4 3 2 1

Contents

Preface

Life goes on; multitudes suffer and perish. Approximately half a million people died in Iraq of war-related causes between 2003 and mid-2011 (Hagopian et al. 2013). An estimated 560,000 persons have been killed in Syria's civil war since 2011 (Haaretz and Reuters 2018). Between 150 million and 1 billion people have been killed in wars throughout recorded history (Hedges 2003). At least 108 million people were killed in wars during the twentieth century alone. Millions of girls, women, boys, and men have been raped in war, including those who have survived and those who have not (Féron 2018; Wolfe 2015). More than 75,000 people are known to have died attempting to migrate since 1996 (Migration Data Portal 2021). Colonialism has killed tens of millions of indigenous people through direct violence and disease (Cook 1998; Stannard 1992). An estimated 7 million people die each year from diseases caused by air pollution (WHO 2018a). An estimated 829,000 people die each year from diarrhea due to scarcity of clean water (WHO 2019). Climate change will have caused, at an accelerating rate over the course of the twenty-first century, premature human deaths at least in the hundreds of thousands (WHO 2018b). Fifteen million adolescent girls reported having experienced forced sex, based on data from 2005 through 2016 (UNICEF 2017). It is estimated that more than 40 million persons were enslaved on any given day in 2016 (International Labour Office 2017). Approximately 69.4 billion land animals were killed for meat in 2013, and estimates for the number of fish killed are in the trillions (ConsiderVeganism.com 2019). More than half of the world's population of nonhuman vertebrate animals have been killed since 1970 (Ingraham 2014).

Flagrant horrors past and present should not overshadow a less palpable truth, which is that harm is *signified* before, during, and after it is perpetrated.[1] It is rendered in discourse. Harm's discourses appeal and appease; they assign blame, minimize harm, or formulate the bases for its legitimacy. They reduce targets, characterizing them in terms of narrow interests or denying that targets have interests uniquely their own (Presser 2013). Harm's discourses include the apocalyptic tale that justifies war in terms of catastrophic threats to a nation's integrity (Smith 2005) and myths that deem sexual violence "not that bad" (Gay 2018). They also include the silences, denials, and rationalizations that hastened the spread of the deadly COVID-19 infection that has ravaged the world as of the early 2020s.

The discursive underpinnings of harm—targets reduced, actors authorized, actions legitimized, in turn mobilizing participation and cultivating indifference to actions' harmful consequences—rely fundamentally on absences. Harm takes shape in and through the ambient and the taken-for-granted. This book is concerned with injuries founded on not saying things. It sets out methods for determining what goes unexpressed to harmful effect.

Consider calls to violence where the targets are referred to as "animals." The reference presupposes but does not say that (nonhuman) animals are harmworthy. The phantom text—the unsaid—matters: without it the message does not point clearly to the legitimacy of harm.[2] Unsaid legitimizes certain types of injury without exposing itself to scrutiny. (I use *unsaid* as a noun throughout this book.) The notion that "it is all right to harm animals" might give pause to those who are invested in widely proclaimed and widely held moral constraints against harm-doing. That is, if social texts spoke more boldly than they do, they would put audiences on alert. Verbal backing for atrocities thus requires not saying words like *atrocity*, not saying what is complex or sympathetic about the target, and not detailing what is depraved or irresponsible about complicity. Meanings packaged in coded fashion also insulate communicators from accountability: they cannot be sanctioned for what they did not precisely say. Thus, tacit communication both allows and sustains harm-doing and injustice.

Another important and vast realm of unsaid is the exclusion and silencing of subordinated beings and their perspectives and circumstances. Some among us are marginalized. Their experiences are ignored; their viewpoints are silenced. Such silencing is both a tool and an effect of power (Russell 2019). As such, silence has a tendency to get fixed in place.

Discourse is implicated in relations of power from an array of major social theoretical perspectives.[3] Gaps in discourse are so implicated as well. Thus, power positions will be a central focus of this book, and their dismantling a main goal. News media seeking profit induce audiences to invest in their own poor health (Stibbe 2004) and emotional insecurity. Politicians striving for (more) power jeopardize the interests of people and other beings. Violence perpetrators rationalize and achieve tolerance for what they do. A variety of destructive outcomes, rooted in power, are sustained by unsaid. Therefore, I do not believe that researchers should only analyze what sits in front of them. But this presents an obvious difficulty: how can analysts pinpoint what is not overtly expressed?

There can be no mere "gathering up" of omissions. It is not feasible nor is it theoretically meaningful to do so. To determine what exists and has force in the world—even as "it" is not exactly "there"— is a fraught business indeed. It would seem to be the same business that cultists, conspiracy theorists, and scientific fact-doubters are engaged in, and closer to religion than to social science. But unsaid analysis is not a trust-your-heart endeavor. It is painstaking; it follows demonstrable steps. It lays bare its premises. It relies on careful methodology along with a bold attitude toward presences and absences. The book seeks to deliver the former and trusts that the reader brings the latter.

Acknowledgments

My thanks go to many.

The Ruth Landes Memorial Research Fund, the Fulbright Finland Foundation, the Fulbright U.S. Scholar Program, and the University of Tennessee's Office of Research & Engagement and Department of Sociology provided essential material support for my research and leave. The Institute of Advanced Studies at University College London and the Faculty of Social Sciences at Tampere University hosted me and gave invaluable opportunities for developing this work.

At Tampere University, I thank Juho Saari, Marjo Silvala, Noora Ellonen, Matti Hyvärinen, Turo-Kimmo Lehtonen, Anna Sofia Salonen, Päivi Honkatukia, Atte Oksanen, students in the Interdisciplinary Narrative Analysis seminar, Narrare: Centre for Interdisciplinary Narrative Studies, Mari Hatavara, Maria Mäkelä, Anna Kuutsa, Kim Schoofs, Laura Kartunnen, Laura Lalu, and Hanna Heino. Thanks also to the scholars at the Institute of Advanced Social Research at Tampere University for their input. At

Fulbright Finland, my thanks go to Terhi Mölsä, Emmi Jelekäinen, and Leasa Weimer, and also Charlie Mathies.

Thanks to the Institute of Criminology and Legal Policy (Krimo) at the University of Helsinki and to the University of Turku Faculty of Law for productive visits. Specific thanks go to Maiju Tanskanen, Elsa Saarikkomäki, and Janne Kivivuori, and to Anne Alvesalo-Kuusi, Johanna Niemi, Heini Kainulainen, and Mirkka Ruotsalainen.

At the Institute of Advanced Studies, UCL, I thank Catherine Stokes, Tamar Garb, Andrew Dean, Mary Rawlinson, and Jakob Stougaard-Nielsen. At Goldsmiths, University of London, I thank Jennifer Fleetwood. At the University of Bristol, I thank Christina Pantazis.

Thanks to Roy Sablosky, Sarah D'Onofrio, Grady Lowery, and Alex Szmutko for research and editing assistance, to Lauren Hill and Laura Silvala for childcare, and to Maura Roessner, Jeff Anderson, and Madison Wetzell for expert guidance at the University of California Press. I am grateful for prodigious ideas from Randy Fromm, Stephen Frosh, Cody Mejeur, Sam McIntyre, and Joachim Savelsberg. Thanks to the anonymous reviewers who also shaped the work.

I am very grateful to my children, Halen and Ansel Presser, whose love, spirited generosity, and enthusiasm for adventure make my work possible and my life joyful.

The book is dedicated to the memory of my cousin Michelle Rosen and my student and friend Gina Benedict.

1 Kept Quiet

The National Embryo Donation Center is a nonprofit organization in the United States whose stated mission is "to protect the lives and dignity of human embryos" by facilitating the adoption of embryos. (Embryo transfer could lead to pregnancy.) It happens to be located in my city of Knoxville, Tennessee. When I first became interested in having children, years ago, I learned that I was excluded from the center's services because I was single. The question "Who can adopt?" posted among the NEDC website's Frequently Asked Questions is answered with a one-sentence statement followed by a bulleted list of eight restrictive criteria. The statement is, "We work hard to assure our donors that their embryos will be placed in healthy, stable homes with loving parents." The first criterion is, "Couples must be a genetic male and a genetic female married for a minimum of 3 years." No explanation is given for this placement restriction. Common-sense reasoning connects "a minimum of 3 years" of marriage back to "stable homes with loving parents." The longevity of the marriage arguably indicates that the household is stable and the parents are loving. But why married? (Why the sanction of the state?) Why genetic male and genetic female? Why male and female? Why couples? Reasons for these provisos are unavailable within the text. For understanding, the reader must consult some unstated, extratextual logic, which is, I venture: married, heterosexual cisgender couples are normal, adequate, and proper (would-be) parents while various other people are not. The fact that this logic is not articulated reflects its dominance and helps sustain its impact.

This book proceeds from an understanding that what is not said does foundational work for the sake of harmful social arrangements. Unsaid *does, invites,* and *conceals* harm. The aims of the book are to draw attention to the effects of unsaid on harm and to advance a methodological approach for determining what is unsaid within texts, particularly where unsaid matters to well-being. Generically I call the approach *unsaid analysis.*

Analyzing what is not said is tricky business indeed. All communication excludes. To make a point, communicators "leave out" far more—incalculably more—than they "put in." In writing that last sentence, I did not write about the changing seasons or my most recent meal. I wrote "communicators" and not "speakers," "agents," or "people." Arguably these "unsaid" things are banal. The things I have in mind, however, are exclusions that matter for social justice and well-being.

Critical scholars from numerous fields—critical race theory; feminist, postcolonial, queer, and disability studies; and ecolinguistics, to name a few—observe that beyond material arrangements, discursive processes—including discursive erasures—produce and reflect relations of power. People are silent, either by virtue of their oppression—in which case they are said to be silenced—or by virtue of their position of power, and in order to maintain such power. Even unintentionally and unaware, people carry forward exclusions that are collectively based (Jalbert 1994). A broad social scientific and activist literature recognizes the understatement of hegemonic logics and the exclusion of oppositional logics as co-constructive of power arrangements and harm. Elaborating how the exclusions and exclusionary understandings can systematically be discovered makes an important contribution to social research and activism. The field of unsaid analysis has been pioneered and developed by literary scholars, communication analysts, linguists, philosophers, sociologists, and psychologists. A criminological/zemiological perspective provides new theoretically informed tools for discerning what is unsaid.[1]

Yet, unsaid is no mere academic concern. Not only researchers, but also laypersons, often suspect that some text is "coded"—that it contains some "subtext." They believe that the subtext achieves something that is socially consequential, specifically that it obscures or supports some misconduct. Coded communication includes "dog whistles" that disseminate hateful messages with presumed intention and often as a signal to committed haters of where the communicator stands. Also coded are understandings of right relations that are simply, perhaps innocently, taken for granted. Left implicit, unsaid is shielded from critique. A cohesive strategy for identifying these sorts of unsaid things in a systematic fashion has been lacking. This book develops such a strategy as a contribution to the critical social research and activism toolkit.

The next section of this introductory chapter sets out the many ways in which power, mainly dominance but also resistance, is wielded via unsaid. I then describe the ideas and theories that inform my methodology.

POWER, HARM, AND UNSAID

Power, harm, and unsaid are variously connected. The voices of the powerless are excluded from, and silenced in, myriad social spaces, which reinforces their powerlessness. Across power positions, one may censor what one says or veil it somehow in order to gain advantage and/or avoid social sanctions for provoking or facilitating harm. The powerful gain and maintain considerable power by keeping quiet.

Speakers Excluded, Speech Repressed

Obstacles to speaking are materially and culturally structured at multiple levels of social engagement. Silence helps some achieve their purposes and causes others to suffer. It is woven into and serves social divisions. Numerous institutions and domains of social life differentially impose silence.

Social positions confer or withhold epistemic authority. Hedges and Fishkin (1994, 3), in reviewing the work of Tillie Olsen, reflect on how "being born into the wrong class, race, or sex, being denied education, becoming numbed by economic struggle, muffled by censorship, or distracted or impeded by the demands of nurturing" create unequal patterns of voice. That is, stratification determines epistemic authority in terms of being too bogged down to speak and in terms of speech being deemed differentially important or tellable. In Western society, the preferred tellers of illness stories have been physicians (Frank 1995). In Western courtrooms professionals are supposed to speak on behalf of the actual parties to conflict (Christie 1977). Generally, persons who are not white, not male, not heterosexual, and not cisgender, and who are poor, cognitively atypical, and "young" or "old," have been discredited. Stigmas associated with some putative trait or conduct also limit standing. Criminalized youth, for example, are compelled to silence in institutional spaces:

> It is often to a young person's detriment to speak in court, because their pleas of innocence, attempts to explain themselves, or their expressions of change may actually hurt their legal defense. Thus, many defense attorneys, and even judges, will stop young people from speaking in court, except at moments when their speech may be safe, for example, during an allocution at a guilty plea, or when young people can describe their compliance with treatment. (Cox 2017, 90)

In everyday life, elites talk too much and prevent others from talking. They establish the rules for communication, set the agenda, summarize "main" points, and otherwise take control linguistically and tonally. The powerful arbitrate the credibility of (the speech of) less powerful communicators. The latter (would-be) communicators are effectively silenced: they have trouble entering or staying in or at the center of conversation.[2] Reductive labels and jokes can silence as well. They do so by negating the diversity of the group, and by denying targets their authority and expertise. "Angry women" who "persist" merit being ignored.[3]

People are silenced depending on what they might say. Authoritarian regimes characteristically impose silence. Among other things, criticisms of the government and accounts of particular injustices, of the present as well as the past, must not be conveyed in speech or writing; penalties can be severe. Notably, authoritarian regimes may also impose speech requirements, such as to praise the country's leaders or a particular god. This pattern—prohibiting some speech, ordering other speech—will become relevant in chapter 2, where the dialectic of too much and too little said is exploited methodologically.

Even under conditions of democracy, particular topics cannot be openly discussed; particular stories cannot be told. Waxman (2003) points to contemporary scholars' tendency to ignore women's stories of the Holocaust to the extent that they are morally complex, not gender-normative, and/or not redemptive. They diverge from the official story of Holocaust victimization—from its "master narrative." Gair and Moloney (2013) dispel the idea that narratives that diverge from the official story are always embraced by progressive audiences. Moloney shared her experience of relinquishing a child to adoption in an article she submitted to a qualitative research journal: the submission received unfavorable reviews. She described "a lingering perception that beneath theselogical criticisms, the intense emotional pain described in my article was too personal and too confronting, and that my counter narrative from the dark underbelly of adoption fell outside the exclusion zone" (56). Similarly, the "chaos narratives" of chronically ill people are hard for other people to hear, noncompliant as they are with dominant narrative expectations, including conventionalized life and story trajectories of triumph, progress, and redemption (Frank 1995). These observations testify to the historical and cultural situatedness of acceptable stories.

Some experiences cannot be spoken of, at least not for a time. The forces behind such silences are complex. They are both external and internal(ized). Many forms and instances of victimization go unrecognized, even unnamed. They are collectively and individually repressed. Examples include state torture, domestic violence, and various forms of sexual violence, including the sexual dimension of other violence. Victims' accounts—sometimes more than the acts of victimization themselves—are forbidden, discouraged, sanctioned, and/or trivialized. To speak would be to threaten current orders and the norms that maintain them: the would-be narratives are unnarratable (Prince 1988, 1).

Or victims may be "at a loss for words." Das and Nandy (1985) observe that victims of atrocity may suffer a "loss of signification" in that "violence cannot be contained within any structure of ideas" (194; see also Bar-On 1999; Welz 2016). Survivors have "a limited capacity of any narrative resources to convey the profundity of the traumatic experiences" (Schwartzmann 2015, 285). The story cannot begin to capture the breadth or strangeness of the experience. What is more, "the survivor's own shame can restrict disclosure" (284). Shame, a form of self-blame, is nurtured by outside forces, yet it is also arguably a means of coping, as one reaches for some meaning for suffering, or sense of justice in the world. Yet, a worry that others "might think it's your fault" ("it" being racist treatment, for example) can inhibit speech (research participant Robertson, quoted in Sheriff 2000, 124). Or, survivors may fear that disclosure will be sanctioned by still-corrupt agents, including formal authorities; victims might then bury their allegations.

Atrocity scholars have shown that silence can be part of a broad societal project of denial (Cohen 2001), one that functions at multiple levels of social life (Savelsberg 2021). Knowledge of violence, its impacts, how it is defined, and the fact that it persists have all been subject to repression, backed by more violence. Beyond genocidal regimes, at a meso level, silence can be coerced by the threat of blackmail or extralegal violence—think of punishment by crime syndicates—and job dismissal or demotion in retaliation for complaining of mistreatment or calling it out (whistleblowing). But also, quite legal institutional mechanisms (e.g., the nondisclosure agreement) exist for suppressing what could be said.

At the same time, silence may be normative, which is to say that it need not be coerced. Sheriff (2000) coins the expression "cultural censorship" to describe a collective prohibition on discussing racism in Brazil, notwithstanding the race consciousness of Brazilians of African descent. She writes: "In Brazil, the subject of racism is circumscribed not only by evasive rhetorical strategies but also by historically rooted, customary silences" (121). Unsaid is broadly structured, but individual speakers opt in. They avoid talking about racism in an attempt to forget it or avoid its emotional sting. Cultures of silence, and fear of the consequences of breaking the silence, foster the passivity of bystanders in the face of harm (Hallsworth and Young 2008; Manji, Presser, and Dickey 2014).

Silence, Voice, and Resistance

Silencing compounds subjugation and suffering for those directly affected. It keeps oppressive structures in place. It also results in lost contributions and incomplete and inaccurate social histories. Speech—call it testimony—can be resistance. We can begin to mount opposition and intervention when we name unjust circumstances, their impacts, and their sources/perpetrators. James Baldwin (1976, 11) thus observed: "The victim who is able to articulate the situation of the victim has ceased to be a victim: he or she has become a threat." To speak the truth of victimization is to begin to upset the power arrangements that have made the victimization possible. It is an expression of power, however rudimentary.

However, silence can also strengthen one's position (Givhan 2020). Simmel (1906, 466) observed that secrecy "confers power to modify fortunes, to produce surprises, joys, and calamities."[4]

Choosing silence can be a tool of resistance—a denunciation of a system of epistemic oppression (Carter 2006), an attempt to reestablish the "ordinariness" of one's daily life in the face of violent disruption (Fleetwood 2019), a "regenerative force" (Godart 2016), or a refusal to participate in one's own subjugation, hence "the right to remain silent" when state agents might interrogate. Poor Brazilians of African descent spoke to Sheriff (2000) of their silence about racism as adaptive, "directed toward protecting oneself and one's intimates from protracted anger and the festering of emotional pain" (125). Though chosen, this silence was an accommodation to things as they are.

During research or institutional interviews, participants' silence, in general or after a specific question, can be a bid to challenge stigmatization or the questioner's authority (Bengtsson and Fynbo 2018; Charmaz 2002). Wherever voice is demanded, silence is protest. Not speaking, like other deliberate not-doings, can be a relatively safe strategy of resistance (Kärki 2018). One tends to "get in trouble" for doing, less often for not doing. Also, one might tactically exploit an unseen and unheard position, as slaves do in waging revolts and vagrant people do in evading the police. Invisibility can confer considerable logistical advantages in struggles against injustice. Codes of silence can facilitate various endeavors and struggles.

Silence can be used strategically. Bhattacharya (2009, 370–71) observes that the use of silence by violated women in Lahaul, India, "is not some kind of pure political resistance—it is compromised, negotiated, and yet powerful enough that within it is contained the possibility of activism, feminist critique of honor and sexuality, and actual practical changes with regard to different forms of violence against women." Still, the choice to stay quiet can be problematic.

The silent party alone may be aware of the intention to protest, which is to say that the protest may not register with oppressors and others. Then, silence may be taken as indifference, ineptitude, or even consent. "Not speaking can entail accepting someone else's story about what happened to you" (Winter 2010, 8). Silence by and large speaks less precisely than voice. Thus it is a precarious strategy for the put-upon and oppressed. It may not even give the *feeling* of power that voice does. Poet Audre Lorde (1997) relates:

> and when we speak we are afraid
> our words will not be heard
> nor welcomed
> but when we are silent
> we are still afraid

Absences within Texts

Houston and Kramarae (1991, 389) astutely observe that "the power to silence another is not simply the power to *prevent* her talk; it is also the power to *shape and control* her talk, to restrict the things that she may talk about and the ways she is permitted to express them, to permit her to speak, but to suppress her authentic voice" (emphases in the original). Beyond persons being altogether silenced or choosing silence, a variety of things that persons might say go missing from texts.[5] Much would-be speech is censored, formally or informally, generally or conditionally—that is to say, at certain times and in certain social settings.

Again, social position directs such absences. Concealment is bound to power positions; (some) power is altogether necessary to achieve absences in the first place. Institutional power—that of governments, media corporations, schools, and so forth—is in part the power to omit. The Russian government, with Vladimir Putin at the helm, criminalized the sharing of "false information" about the Russian invasion of Ukraine that began February 24, 2022. This included calling the war a war. The penalties were harsh, including prison terms up to fifteen years. No other body could suppress speech quite so absolutely as the government.

As previously discussed, we censor *ourselves* for strategic reasons—simply to get along or to advance our interests. Savelsberg (2020), who studied family histories written by children and grandchildren of the German Holocaust perpetrator generation, observed that many people in the older generation disclosed their past activity or passivity *vis-à-vis* the Holocaust selectively in order to manage stigma and shame. Their descendants kept the silence for similar reasons or to protect their relationships with their elders. But self-censorship is more quotidian than that example implies.

Arguably more benign is so-called discretion or tact. Social norms and settings demand, and selectively enforce, tact. (The social norms that make these demands are themselves often unspoken.) Politeness may inspire indirect, and thus supposedly not-so-informative, utterances (Thomas 1995). Ambiguous comments routinely take the place of direct criticism. Tact may furthermore inspire outright silence, in response to something said, in lieu of outright disagreement. In these cases, unsaid supports interactants' positive self-image (Goffman 1955, 1959). Indirect expression thus can be quite normative, with straightforward expression the deviant kind.[6]

What is worthwhile or advisable to say is altogether bound to social context. We limit what we say depending on the circumstance. For example, different situations call for different amounts of sharing about oneself. What "should be said" also varies with historical period in a society as well as across societies. Cultural groups differ in how directly or indirectly they communicate. Then there are cultural taboos, which forbid actions including speech actions. An example is the taboo in many societies against discussing or even mentioning certain bodily functions.

Taboos are powerful means of so-called informal social control. Not-saying is also formal, enforced by governments. Subjugated persons may be compelled to say certain things, such as to signify their obedience and "reform." Prisoners in China and the United States, for example, have been made to recite their moral transformation from waywardness in a way that validates particular institutional expectations (Fox 1999; Zhang and Dong 2019). Similarly, states coerce criminal confessions through means that are both licit (e.g., plea bargains) and illicit (e.g., torture). "The oppression of speech exists right alongside the oppression of silence" (Gullette 2017, 185). The subaltern has been made to say that which accommodates the other's position of control, while leaving out that which might threaten that position. This is not to say that the subject does not get anything from the subjection. They may get less horrible treatment or early release from confinement. Ginio (2010), in examining the situation of Africans who fought for France, observes that their complicity with a narrative that occludes violence on behalf of colonial power may reflect a desire for some place in French history.

For elites, silence on a baneful or controversial action is a prerogative, and often a strategy, for acquiring and maintaining power.[7] Leaving things unsaid can help communicators avoid criticism and accountability. Hence the ambiguous orders to perpetrate violence such as crime-syndicate "bosses," genocidaires, and other political leaders are known to dispense. Goffman (1959, 62) observed: "Communication techniques such as innuendo, strategic ambiguity, and crucial omissions allow the misinformer to profit from lies without, technically, telling any." Keeping quiet or speaking in coded fashion may accompany explicit denials of morally troublesome conduct and/or its effects.

Even in saying *something* about our troublesome conduct and its effects, we leave things out. We tailor our message so that our actions sound relatively benign or, if not, so that we come across as minimally culpable. Power shapes the capacity to withhold information from others (Zerubavel 2006, 39). Selective or ambiguous speech is a tool of power. Politicians use oblique or otherwise ambiguous expressions to describe situations for which they might bear some responsibility (e.g., "collateral damage" rather than "killing"). George Orwell (1968, 136) observed that obfuscation is an important strategy leaders use to communicate about "the indefensible" and thus avoid raising alarm:

> Things like the continuance of British rule in India, the Russian purges and deportations, the dropping of the atom bombs on Japan, can indeed be defended, but only by arguments which are too brutal for most people to face, and which do not square with the professed aims of political parties. Thus political language has to consist largely of euphemism, question-begging and sheer cloudy vagueness.

The news media uphold power structures by adopting euphemisms favorable to elites and elite rule: for example, attributing "misstatements" rather than "lies" to politicians at the highest levels (Bauder 2018; see also deMause 2020). Even minute exclusions reflect and substantiate power positions. Consider differential use of race terms for people, such that, as bell hooks (1981, 138) observed, "the word woman is synonymous with white woman." The word *animal* is synonymous with the nonhuman kind; humans' animality requires special comment (Singer 1990). Status quo power relations are linguistically coded as standard, and dominant beings are coded as central in the moral scheme of things (Butler 2004, Opotow 1993). Zerubavel (2019) similarly points out the *nonuse* of words for that which is normalized, such as *heteroerotic*, in contrast to the deviantized and therefore marked *homoerotic*. Supposedly normal life is "semiotically superfluous" (64–65).

One of the foremost exclusions of elite communication is the communicator's own position,[8] meaning both their identity and their stake in what they are saying. Who is speaking? Why are they speaking? What interests are being served by their speaking? The scholarly claim to objectivity traditionally implies that the scholar's only interests are to create knowledge and perhaps to be of some real-world use. Critical scholars call out the hollowness of that implication and furthermore turn objectivity on its head. Criminologist Biko Agozino (2003, 163) defines objectivity not as "positionlessness but . . . as the procedure of taking a position without concealing or distorting oppositions to the position taken." Agozino and other critical scholars make plain their own commitments in doing scholarly work.

In addition to their own positionality and interests, elite communicators exclude potential counterarguments to, or problems with, what they say. Or, they include the arguments and problems but minimize the challenges these pose. The work of excluding is a kind of art for public relations specialists such as speechwriters and marketing executives.

Selective communication fails to give a full and authentic picture of some phenomenon. It might be countered that the charge of obfuscation wrongly presumes that a full and authentic picture is possible. Or, it could be said that we cannot know what the speaker knows, and therefore that the charge is unfair. I take the point that "what there is to know" of other minds (and all else) is indeterminate. Still, these criticisms strike me as pedantic. It has been revealed time and again, across political regimes and epochs, that there *was* more to reveal and that authorities knew things that they kept hidden. I have many times in my life kept some fuller awareness *from* myself, a feat I only recognized later on. I did so—it occurs to me now—to avoid some emotional pain, including the pain of knowing about harm-doing in which I was implicated. But also, I did not know all that was knowable from my particular vantage. Whereas the words *obfuscate* and *obscure* seem to imply intent, the speaker's intent to conceal information is far less important than the fact that information is concealed impactfully.

Omissions and Ignorance

We speak in ways that omit; we may not even be aware of the omissions. The question arises: How can we lack such awareness?

We avoid knowing. We ignore information that would contradict our existing ideas, including but not limited to ideas about self. Festinger's (1957) cognitive dissonance theory offers an explanation.

Cognitive dissonance is unease due to holding conflicting ideas. It motivates action to reduce the dissonance. In line with the theory, Swann, Johnson, and Bosson (2009, 84) state: "When people receive feedback that challenges their self-views, they behaviorally resist such challenges, and such resistance activity stabilizes their self-views." Resistance, of course, includes not-doings, like disattention. Narayan, Case, and Edwards (2011, 5) observe: "Most people seek out information which agrees with their current world-view and cognitive skill levels rather than acknowledge or seek new information that causes an uncomfortable conflict in their minds." They asked 34 study participants to record information-related thoughts and activities in daily journals over a period of five months.

> Participants' information journals revealed that although they were generally looking for more rather than less information on topics that interested them in their everyday lives, there were certain areas where they actively avoided information. These were specific issues with which the participants either had some previous experience or knowledge or wanted to avoid any new information that might interfere with their decisions or current way of thinking. It was a way of maintaining the *status quo* or not rocking the boat. This was noticed mainly in the following areas: financial affairs, certain medical issues, religious issues, and certain political issues. (4)

Hence, our statements may be missing something because we lack information, and we may lack information because we have steered clear of it. This ignorance is active and willful: "they do not know and they do not want to know" (Tuana 2006, 10; see also Gross and McGoey 2015).[9] The desire not to know points to some measure of knowing *in* not-knowing. On that view Cohen (2001, 24) observes that denial "allows for the strange possibility of simultaneously knowing and not-knowing." Cohen deploys psychoanalytic theory in describing such denial, as in the subject has an "unconscious need not to know about troubling matters" (24), although he also emphasizes the social support that bystanders to harm in particular receive for remaining ignorant.

Whereas individuals often have personal reasons to be uninformed, then—for instance, a patient opting to learn less than there is to know about their medical condition—knowledge avoidance is an indelibly communal phenomenon.[10] "Whole societies have unmentioned and unmentionable rules about what should not be openly talked about" (Cohen 2001, 45). The cognitive communities of which we are members set out what we should or need to know and what we should or need *not* to know. Thus Zerubavel (2006, 23) observes that "ignoring something is more than simply failing to notice it. Indeed, it is quite often the result of some pressure to actively disregard it. Such pressure is usually a product of social norms of attention designed to separate what we conventionally consider 'noteworthy' from what we come to disregard as mere background 'noise.'"

Nowhere is ignorance so patently socially organized as it is concerning racialized positions and interests (Mills 2007, 2015). Mills (2015, 219) takes note of the concept of color-blind racism that Bonilla-Silva theorized, "in which whites deny any racism, declare their support of nondiscriminatory liberal norms and ideals, but simultaneously decry the unwillingness to work, preference for living on welfare, culture of poverty, and/or refusal to assimilate of particular nonwhite groups." In a revision of that concept, he writes: "The real heart of white ignorance today, whether accompanied by such prejudicial characterizations or not, is the refusal to recognize how the legacy of the past, as well as ongoing practices in the present, continues to handicap people of color now granted nominal and juridical and social equality." This ignorance is systematic, as seen for example in schools' miseducation of young people on how race operates historically and in the present day (Brunsma, Brown, and Placier 2012; Chandler and McKnight 2009). Privilege, which "appears as the fabric of life, as the way things are" (Wildman and Davis 1995, 883), gives people an emotional stake in the ignorance.

Textual absences are reciprocally related to harm, generally mediated by blocking harm or its antecedents from view. We cannot address what is "not there." Ronald Reagan "was president for nearly five years before he said the word 'AIDS' in public, nearly seven years before he gave a speech on a health crisis that would go on to kill more than 650,000 Americans and stigmatize even more" (La Ganga 2016). AIDS activists recognized the violence of not-saying and coined the slogan, "Silence equals death" (Finkelstein 2018). Naming a problem is a co-requisite to treating it as one.

INSPIRATIONS FOR UNSAID ANALYSIS

Absences of stunning variety assemble life as we know it. How to track them down? Jeff Ferrell (2018, 190) observes: "Absence may be present, but knowing how to notice it, record it, and account for it is another matter." Ferrell had in mind all manner of exclusions from modern society but especially exclusion of persons compelled to "drift" in social space. The task of tracking down absences is no less daunting if we restrict the focus to *textual* absences. The things unsaid, unheard, or unseen, such as on the page or the electronic screen, are incalculable. What is said is simply what is fore-grounded—dark on light; what is not said is everything else. The purpose of this book is to set out a method for discerning absences in texts.[11] I wrote the book because I perceived the need for rigor in determining what is unsaid in discourse for the sake of critical social research. I agree with Watts (1997, 112) that silence "deserves to be given as much interpretive attention as talk."

A focused program of research on unsaid has been gaining momentum, with incisive monographs (Jaworski 1993; Schröter 2013) and edited volumes (Jaworski 1997; Murray and Durrheim 2019a; Schröter and Taylor 2018; Tannen and Saville-Troike 1985). "We might say that the social sciences and humanities have taken a turn toward silence," write Murray and Durrheim (2019b, 7). A somewhat older literature on silence in interpersonal exchanges is largely but not exclusively attentive to "literal silences" (Billig and

Marinho 2007)—not speaking at all, if only for a short while (Kurzon 1998). In contrast, the unsaid program, and this book which is part of it, concern not speaking about some things when speaking about other things, what Kurzon (2007) calls thematic silence and Billig and Marinho (2007) call metaphorical silence.

It can seem mischievous to entify unsaid. But it is not extraordinary. Social actors themselves recognize the beingness of absences within speech. In popular culture silence is figured as "deafening" or something that can "be cut with a knife." Human rights activists refer to "walls of silence" (i.e., among police) and "breaking the silence." Scholars, too, discuss present-day suffering, grounded in current practices and past savagery, in terms of "shadows" (Briggs and Gamero 2017) and "shadowlands" (Matsuoka and Sorenson 2001) and, more evocatively still, "ghosts," "haunting," and "spectralities" (Blanco and Peeren 2013; Fisher 2014; Gordon 1997; Matsuoka and Sorenson 2001). Butalia (2000) refers to "layers of silence" attendant on the violence associated with the partition of India. For Abbott (2013, 22–23), a "palpable unknown" is "a hole in the narrative that travels through it and stays in the mind afterward." Surely the move to treat what is not said as a *thing* is rhetorical, but it is not without precedent. By no means did I invent it. Moreover, it is no more rhetorical than treating what *is* said as a thing. Both represent processes of communication as physical objects.

Whereas I take the mischief of language as inspiration, I am ultimately keen to shed light on solemn things—actions and patterns that cause suffering and injustice. Particular textual absences sustain power relations and cause harm. They do so by downplaying nefarious actions and arrangements, absenting alternative perspectives, and obscuring the realities whereby some beings are marginalized and harmed. That is why the project of determining textual absences presumes and even requires an interested analyst—one with ideas about what *ought* to be said but is not. The analyst must make those ideas plain. But reflexivity is only a start, if an essential one. Something more technical is required.

Just a few moments' contemplation makes clear that texts make meaning only insofar as they *exclude*. "Selecting information, be it for encoding or retrieving, means rejecting and excluding other information—information deemed to be obscured, repressed or forgotten" (Brockmeier 2002, 22). Saying not only entails but *necessitates* not-saying. The idea that textual exclusions are endemic to communication is developed in various highly influential social theories. Poststructuralist thinking in general is focused on absence (Fuery 1995). Derrida's concept of hauntology centers on missingness, as Fisher (2014, 17–18) explains:

> Hauntology was the successor to previous concepts of Derrida's such as the trace and *différance*; like those earlier terms, it referred to the way in which nothing enjoys a purely positive existence. Everything that exists is possible only on the basis of a whole series of absences, which precede and surround it, allowing it to possess such consistency and intelligibility that it does. In the famous example, any particular linguistic term gains its meaning not from its own positive qualities but from its difference from other terms.

Psychoanalysts following Freud have also been greatly concerned with absence. Freud assigned commanding roles to missing and distant things—the absence of the object of one's desire, the lack of a penis, and the repression (i.e., forced retreat) of disturbing thoughts. Manifest behavior (e.g., obsessive conduct) reflects unseen functions. Hints of the unseen functions may be communicated, but stealthily: it is the work of the psychoanalyst to decipher them. Moving beyond Freud, Lacan connected absence and language. Inspired by Saussure's linguistics and specifically the idea of meaning as always relational, Lacan (1977, 65) considered "the word" as "a presence made of absence." Stockholder (1998, 405) explains Lacan's thinking:

> Meaning arises not from positive or freestanding ideas and concepts, but only from the systematic differences that constitute them. If meaning resides in a system of differences, and differences are kinds of nothings, empty spaces, as it were, then our sense of meaning arises

out of gaps, emptiness, voids that we spend our days vainly trying to paper over.

If not saying things is fundamental to making meaning, then criticism on the basis of what is unsaid runs the risk of absurdity. The unsaid analysis that is needed is guided by theory and, furthermore, is rigorous, shareable, and accountable to empirical observation.

FRAMING THE METHODOLOGY

Vincent (2010, 49) articulates the fundamental question for any unsaid analytic methodology: "How do we ascribe meaning to silence when all that can be heard is the absence of speech?" For fine-grained insights on the functions and practical mechanics of communicative gaps, I turn to linguistics, specifically pragmatics, and conversation analysis. For insights on the nature and mechanics of harm-genic discursive forms, I turn to critical discourse analysis and narrative studies, especially narrative criminology. The end result of these different forays is a segmented methodology that pays close attention to local norms of communication, including how much to communicate; asymmetries within a text and across texts; recognized linguistic markers of displacement, like metaphor and presupposition; questions of who and what is marginalized within a text; and knowledge of sociopolitical contexts.

Pragmatics and Conversation Analysis

The subfield of linguistics known as pragmatics addresses questions of what actually comes across as meaning within communication (Thomas 1995, 2). A main premise of pragmatics is that more is meant than what is said. The fact that language users imply more than they say, and otherwise tend to pursue efficiency and parsimony, suggests the predictability of missing material.[12]

The work of H. Paul Grice (1975) provides an especially powerful framework for understanding absences in communication. Grice pointed out that conversation has us "implicating" things, trusting our interlocutors to grasp our full message. Such trust is social, not personal, based on the "cooperative principle" governing conversation and a related set of "maxims" that lay out what can be left unspoken. The cooperative principle, which is descriptive and not normative, is: "Make your conversational contribution such as is required, at the stage at which it occurs, by the accepted purpose or direction of the talk exchange in which you are engaged" (45). The maxims, which follow, serve the cooperative principle and fall into four categories: quantity, quality, relation, and manner.

Quantity

Maxim: Make your contribution as informative as is required (for the current purposes of the exchange).
Maxim: Do not make your contribution more informative than is required.

Quality

Supermaxim: Try to make your contribution one that is true.
  Maxim: Do not say that for which you lack adequate evidence.

Relation

Maxim: Be relevant.

Manner

Supermaxim: Be perspicuous.
  Maxim: Avoid obscurity of expression.
  Maxim: Avoid ambiguity.
  Maxim: Be orderly.
  Maxim: Be brief (avoid unnecessary prolixity).

Grice's conversational maxims point to what conversationalists need not and should not say from the perspective of most conventional communicators. For example, because speakers are supposed to say what is true, they need not and should not append to their claims testimonies to the truth of those claims. Because speakers are supposed to be relevant, they should not say things that are off-topic or elaborated unnecessarily. When speakers seem to be "flouting" the maxims, their co-conversationalist will try to figure out what is being implied by the breach.

An important limitation of Grice's theory for present purposes is that it assumes that the primary purpose of conversation is to exchange information (47), with Grice noting that "the scheme needs to be generalized to allow for such general purposes as influencing or directing the actions of others" (47). The theory, in other words, presumes that communicators are trying to communicate, not *miscommunicate* (Hadi 2013).[13] As such, Grice's scheme would actually, and grossly, understate the extent of unsaid. Still, Grice sensitizes us to the fact that social conventions direct us to avoid saying certain things when we are communicating. Interlocutors fill in gaps: they do not presume that utterances should be without them. Moreover, Grice's theory suggests that interlocutors fill in gaps in particular ways. They assume that the communication is true and that the most unambiguous interpretation is the correct one, for instance. These insights will have ramifications for understanding the social construction of textual absences, coming up in chapter 5.

Related to pragmatics in important ways—sharing a focus on the social context of communication, for one thing—is conversation analysis (Drew 2018). Originally conceptualized by Harvey Sacks, conversation analysis takes a "sequential approach to the process or the progression of interaction in real time" (Drew 2018). It takes up unsaid (among other things) as a function of what people say in conversation, when they say those things, and related conventions. For example, when "How are you feeling?" is used in a greeting, Sacks (1989, 238) observed, "it's a breach of the proper forms to begin to launch right then and there into what it is that's bothering you."

However, conventional responses are available for opening up the possibility of elaborating on the trouble, such as "It's a long story," which could prompt invitations such as "I've got time" or "Please go ahead." The socially intelligent speaker waits for such an invitation before proceeding to elaborate. A focus on turns at talk, and specifically on "adjacency pairs" (e.g., the question–answer pair), has implications for evaluating silence, including exactly which co-conversationalist a silence may be said to rightly "belong to."

A sociologically relevant example of conversation analysis and unsaid comes from Kitzinger (2000), who demonstrates the ways in which speakers situate "coming out" as gay within their turn at talk, to keep potentially critical things from being said responsively. "By embedding information about speakers' sexuality in the middle of turn constructional units (TCUs), or in following them with multiple TCUs, speakers protect the recipients from having to produce a response" (187). Kitzinger's research highlights the fact that what might be considered technical speech choices concerning said and unsaid are deployed for social purposes. Here, the way person 1 assembles their speech delays person 2's response, and quite likely shapes the nature of any response at all: it produces something unsaid. It must be noted, however, that the absences that govern deviantized sexualities in the first place are not accessible via linguistics and conversation analysis, in part due to the focus of these fields on discursive agency rather than received gaps. The structures of concern to those fields are fairly local. In contrast, discourse analysis, including the kind that is called critical, does highlight the broader forms, strategies, and social relations that shape communication.

Critical Discourse Analysis

Discourse analysis is also centrally concerned with discursive practices, though not necessarily within conversation. Discourse analysis tends to involve close attention to language in use, including language in written and oral forms. Whereas discourse analysts focus attention on "describing and detailing linguistic features" of texts, critical discourse analysts also ask "*why* and *how* these features are produced and what possible ideological goals they might serve" (Machin and Mayr 2012, 5; emphasis in the original). An unsaid analysis that is oriented toward social harm is properly a project of critical discourse analysis.

Critical discourse analysts undoubtedly recognize the key role of what goes unsaid in social life (Huckin 2002; Luke 2002). Fairclough (1992), who laid much of the groundwork of critical discourse analysis, maintains that the word *critical* "implies showing connections and causes which are hidden" (9). Implicit communication is a common theme of critical discourse analysis. Its practitioners scrutinize absences and abstruseness surrounding authority (Fairclough 1989, 127), agency (Van Leeuwen 1995), conflict (Machin and Mayr 2012, 95), racism (Teo 2000), suffering (Stibbe 2001), and more. They "may examine the style, rhetoric or meaning of texts for strategies that aim at the concealment of social power relations, for instance by playing down, leaving implicit or understating responsible agency of powerful social actors in the events represented in the text" (van Dijk 1993, 250). Thus van Dijk (2014, 258) observes, based on study of a British news article concerning asylum seekers, that "vagueness can be used to attribute negative characteristics to outgroups or to represent the ingroup (such as the taxpayer) as a victim of the outgroup."

Machin and Mayr (2012, 186) note that "language is about concealing as well as revealing." If discourse analysis seems to be focused on what language reveals rather than what it conceals, it may be primarily a function of how analyses are represented or not represented. When (critical or other) discourse analysts explore impersonalization—the passive voice, for example—they are, in effect, exploring the absence of active voice, or agency rendered missing. When discourse analysts examine a use of metaphor, they are, in effect, foregrounding the unstated logic of the metaphor. And so on. I can think of no discourse analytic techniques that do not do the work of pulling unsaid out of the shadows.

However, I believe that a dedicated unsaid analysis adds a novel and furthermore vital dimension to critical discourse analysis. First, the concern of unsaid analysis is hidden meaning generally, not only hidden ideology. It is attentive not just to what is getting smuggled into the text—presuppositions, or the characteristics of a metaphor's source material—but also what is *not* getting in: missing perspectives and contexts, for example. Critical scholars have registered these absences in terms of lack of representation for certain persons. Discourse analysis typically does not ask who is missing at all. In a sense, this kind of missingness is Fairclough's "social practice"— situated in the social surround.[14] The discourse analyst has had no formal strategies for uncovering the subaltern's not-speaking; I want to fill that gap. Second, a dedicated unsaid analysis underscores the exceptional force of discursive exclusion. What is not there is *uniquely* prone to escaping attention. As such, unsaid is crucial to ideology. Third, given the special judiciousness with which analysts must call something out as unsaid, an express unsaid analysis is well warranted. Unsaid analysis needs an especially large measure of care.

Narrative Studies

Whereas things go missing from texts generally, at numerous points throughout the book my empirical focus narrows to narratives or stories.[15] Thus, my development of unsaid analysis is also informed by studies of narrative. This is because stories play a unique role in patterns of harm *and* because they "do" absences in a special and especially impactful way. Stories seem to aspire to full coverage, or as White (1987, 11) writes, "narrative strains for the effect of having filled in all the gaps." And yet, stories are essentially selective on several grounds, not least grounds of power (Plummer 2019). A consideration of what stories are and what they do clarifies their selectivity.

First, though, a brief look at the field of narrative criminology, in which I situate myself, is in order.

NARRATIVE CRIMINOLOGY

Narrative criminology is a domain of narrative scholarship that centers on harm *and* a domain of criminology that centers on narrative. It is a paradigm that frames the study of how stories may promote, or conversely inhibit or combat, harm (Presser 2009; Presser and Sandberg 2015). Its analytical concern is with stories rather than with whatever information those stories may *contain.* The narrative criminologist might, for example, ask who the hero of a salient story is and whether the hero has helpers in the heroic quest. The biographical or contextual details conveyed by the story are not usually of primary interest. Narrative criminology spotlights the constitutive potential of storytelling.

Narrative criminologists ask how stories help sustain terrorism (Presser 2012; Sandberg 2013), party culture (Tutenges and Sandberg 2013), police officer culture (Kurtz and Upton 2017), interpersonal violence (Copes, Hochstetler, and Sandberg 2015; Otto 2020; Presser 2013), and meat-eating and criminal punishment (Presser 2013). They examine corporate communication (Schally 2018), political speech (Barrera 2017), laws (Gathings and Parrotta 2013; Ningard 2018; Offit 2019), and criminological theories (Presser 2018). Stories shape both social reproduction and social transformation, hence narrative criminological research on *resistance* to harm and harming (Brisman 2019; Joosse, Bucerius, and Thompson 2015; Sandberg and Andersen 2019).

Theoretical forerunners of narrative criminology are several (Presser 2016). Within criminology alone they include neutralization theory, labeling theory, constitutive criminology, and structured action theory. Narrative criminology was also inspired by case studies of mass harm in which storied ideologies demonstrably mobilized participation. Narrative criminology has developed a rather broad remit both theoretically and empirically, nurtured by a concern with how whole lives and histories (of individuals and groups) are summoned in claims about and enactments of the (ir)responsible self. Narrative criminologists generally take the view that stories play a special role in our moral and social lives, and exert a special force. These capacities owe to what stories *are*, a central question for narratology. Across disciplines, scholars have also used narratological ideas to clarify what stories *do*.

WHAT STORIES ARE AND WHAT THEY DO

Conceptions of narrative are various. Narrative is quintessentially either a text or "collection of signs" (Prince 1982, 7), a communicative activity (Brockmeier 2004; Phelan 1989; Smith 1981), or a way of thinking (Bruner 1986). Many scholars hold that narratives recount particular events (Abbott 2002; Herman 2009) that unfold over time (Labov and Waletzky 1967; Herman 2009), answering the questions "What happened?" and "Why?" But some scholars conceive of narrative as a form that centers on felt experience, answering the question "What was it like?" (Fludernik 1996; Herman 2009). A common view is that the main, narrated event is a conflict (Prince 2003) or moral disruption of some kind (Bruner 1990). Then, the narrative hones a morally relevant message (Labov and Waletzky 1967; White 1987).

How do stories construct absences? First, stories usually center on events, but only *some* events. Second, stories typically convey a moral position, often obliquely. Third, stories are adaptable, inherently unfixed. Fourth, stories need not be full-blown renderings of events: "small stories" are the kind that merely hint at such. Fifth, stories contain gaps, which has been linked to their emotional power. Sixth, stories may be seen as hegemonic or counter-hegemonic, which cues us to the silencing stories do.

Stories out of events. Stories typically represent events, or delimited happenings in a particular time and place. I define story as an account of an experience of events over time that makes a point.

I join those who use *story* and *narrative* interchangeably, even without highlighting it. Actually, it is quite customary, especially in the humanities, to distinguish between "story" as narrated events and "narrative" (or "narrative discourse") as the report (Abbott 2002; Chatman 1978). This distinction is tied to unsaid.

The Russian formalist school of literary thought differentiates between the *fabula*, "the basic story elements constituting a narrative," and the *sjužet* or discourse—their respective concerns being *what* is told versus *how* it is told (Herman 1995, 30). The *sjužet* cannot and does not exactly, or fully, capture events lived through and actions taken. For one thing, the duration of the discourse in most credible cases differs from the time span of events and actions: hence for example ellipses, or omissions of events from stories (Genette 1980). More generally, and beyond academic conversations, the event, if not our experience of it, is imagined as whole, exhaustive, and verifiable in its original form (White 1980). In contrast, the narrative that tells of an event patently filters out some things and emphasizes others.

In both the cultural imaginary and in literary deconstructions, it is obvious that much goes on that is not storied: much goes unsaid. According to van Hulst (2019, 2), storytellers emplot events "when they select some events for inclusion in the story and ignore others." As stated above, stories are generally told concerning "some sort of disruption or disequilibrium into a storyworld" (Herman 2009, 9), some "deviation from a canonical cultural pattern" (Bruner 1990, 49–50). Conversely, stories are not usually told about that which is deemed routine, predictable, or morally unproblematic. If such stories are told, they tend to be rated as low in tellability or narrativity (Abbott 2002; Herman 2002). And so, the details of events—for instance, the composite moves associated with telling someone "I went out to eat"—are customarily unspoken, in what I refer to as metonymic storytelling (see chapter 3). On the other end of the spectrum, stories may be considered low in tellability when topics are seen as astonishing or indecent (Norrick 2005). In addition, some experiences, such as unrelenting pain, seem to be "beyond words" (Frank 1995; see also Warhol 2005). Nonetheless, and against theories of narrative as necessarily *told* (e.g., Brockmeier

2004), Ricoeur (1991, 30) observes that a "given chain of episodes" in a life that has yet to be recounted may be considered "a story not yet told."

Moral positions. Narratives have a point to make, or as White (1987, 24) put it, "narrativizing discourse serves the purpose of moralizing judgments"; and as Bruner (1990, 51) observed, "to tell a story is inescapably to take a moral stance." Yet, stories regularly make their point surreptitiously: they "keep their principles implied" (Frank 2010, 134). A story I have told of having children contains a moral assessment of what it means to be a parent. In every telling I have left this moral assessment implicit. The presumed moral of a story may be more or less obvious, but it is rarely expressed "in so many words." That stories do not usually come straight out with "the point" is perhaps best illustrated by the fact that readers or audiences regularly disagree on what the point of a novel, film, or performance even *is.* Narrative analysts, following suit, stress the indeterminacy and ambiguity of the stories they study (Polletta 2006; Riessman 2008; Sandberg, Tutenges, and Copes 2015).

Quite often the moral message of stories is conveyed through characters, who act in good and bad ways and have good and bad things happen to them. "In most plots, there are characters who perform actions in pursuit of goals, events that present obstacles to goals, conflicts between characters, clever methods of resolving conflicts, and consequences of these resolutions" (Graesser et al. 2002, 234). Stories cast characters as more or less righteous and as more or less important. Some characters are thickly portrayed in the story, while others receive relatively thin and shallow treatment. At the extreme, thinly treated characters are depicted in a reductive way, with little going on that is self-motivated (Presser 2013). Given space limitations, stories must focus on only some persons, events, and actions. By their very design, then, narratives produce asymmetries of representation. The asymmetries tend to follow culturally approved economies of attention and designations of moral value.

Consider the minority characters cast as sidekicks in films and television shows.

Adaptability. Stories are characteristically adaptable. They are prone to revision, though different versions are widely perceived as the same titular story (Norrick 1997). Consider that people around the world and across tellings recognize "the" Cinderella story, based on the barest of elements. If a particular rendition of "the" story lacks slippers or has a male protagonist or a nonhuman fairy godmother, it may still be readily considered a Cinderella story. Unjust oppression and its glorious overcoming strike me as "the" story's essentials (though others may glean other essentials). So it is too with versions of stories that evidently promote harm, such as that of a greedy, mendacious group working against national interests and spoiling the national culture, who are then targeted for genocide. People seem to know some very influential stories on a basic level.

My main point relating to unsaid, then, is this. For every storyable experience, there are countless ways a story *could* be told. To put it another way, "every story is potentially contestable by multiple alternatives" (Phelan 2008, 168). Polletta (2009, 1506) points out that different versions of a story "navigate similarly between the poles of culturally familiar oppositions." Accordingly, stories lack a stable textual basis, such that "the" story is not precisely said. It is a fleeting idea of a text, more than "a" text itself.

Small stories. Bamberg and Georgakopoulou (2008) have honed *small stories* as "an umbrella term that captures a gamut of underrepresented narrative activities, such as tellings of ongoing events, future or hypothetical events, and shared (known) events, but it also captures allusions to (previous) tellings, deferrals of tellings, and refusals to tell" (381). In effect, small stories leave out basic elements that prototypical stories are said to have. They might mention an event but not articulate what came afterward or what anyone's experience of the event was. They might recount actions but not characters, or describe characters but not actions. They can say something without the "saying" being at all obvious.

Slogans may be conceived of as small stories. "Make America Great Again" (or MAGA for short) was the widely used slogan of Trumpism. Narrativity is suggested by the slogan's dynamism, from great to not great to great once more. But who are its characters? One is the candidate-*cum*-leader, the heroic figure who makes the promise to make America great again: that was Donald J. Trump. Other implied characters are the politicians who preceded Trump and those who presently oppose Trump, along with other people who have sullied America. Slogans such as MAGA are brief by design, which is good for message portability (e.g., to fit the text on caps). They promise to create a big tent of followers (or, in the case of advertising, consumers). The MAGA slogan/small story furthermore leaves implicit the histories and moral characterizations that many would deem racist and xenophobic. The "BLM" slogan, for the Black Lives Matter movement, is less widely recognizable, but likewise a small story. The unsaid is that Black people's lives have not *been* treated as mattering; the text's narrativity stems from that unstated allegation. The slogan/story gains some of its emotional thrust, I contend, from its brevity (Presser 2018).

Gaps, invitation, and emotion. Gaps in fictional texts, of various sorts, invite readers to draw imaginatively on their own experience to interpret the meaning of those texts (Caracciolo 2012). H. Porter Abbott (2013, 107) finds that "gaps are endemic in narrative and have been since people started telling stories." David Herman (2002, 66) states that "narratives involve neither fully open nor fully specified action representations, but rather strategically underspecified ones." According to James Phelan (2017), gaps and ambiguities are resources that authors use for rhetorical purposes.

Mysteries characteristically withhold plot-relevant information—commonly, the identity of a malefactor—until the story's end. But things are left out of stories for the sake of artfulness whatever the genre. Whereas suspenseful plots delay the revelation of something important either happening or being revealed, all good narratives absorb their audiences through carefully edited sequencing and characterization. Stories that did not skip over some events would be tedious. "Stories can be digressed from, abandoned, returned to and unfinished, sometimes quite deliberately and strategically too, for instance, when the teller wants to leave their addressees wanting for more" (De Fina and Georgakopoulou 2012, 111). Prince (1988, 2) conceives of the nonnarrated as something "not told (at least for a while) . . . because of some narrative call for rhythm, characterization, suspense, surprise, and so on." Rather than being compromised by omissions, stories gain lyricism from them.[16]

Stories can move and compel us (Frank 2010). In my 2018 book *Inside Story* I explored the question of what makes some stories uniquely absorbing, with a concern for how they consequently might mobilize mass harm.

> Some narratives are more impactful than others because they instate the moral oppositions and make the identity statements that we favor or at least take for granted, such as concerning our position vis-à-vis others. They install culturally familiar and rewarding versions of ourselves and our lives. (137)

Impactful stories need not be dramatic. They may be rather muted in tone and still affect people, inducing a sense of satisfaction with existing, harmful arrangements which fosters support: consider the public complacency in the face of mass imprisonment. "Stories give comfort to bystanders when others are suffering, by telling us those others are unimportant or deserving of their pains. Stories also satisfy because they position us favorably relative to social or moral inferiors, often through conventional omissions and silences" (139). This too is a kind of seduction; and this seduction is also consequential.

Hegemony and counter-hegemony. Alongside psychologically attuned explorations of how stories impact us, a literature has developed on the political functions of collective stories. Scholars in the latter tradition portray a society that is *inter alia* narratively ordered. Some stories dominate: they reflect and support status quo norms and roles. Narratives that dominate are called hegemonic, dominant, majoritarian, or master narratives. Narratives that oppose these are called subversive or counter-narratives or counter-stories (Bamberg and Andrews 2004; Ewick and Silbey 1995; Halverson, Goodall, and Corman 2011; Solórzano and Yosso 2002). Counter-narratives are said to "bear witness to social relations that the dominant culture tends to deny or minimize" (Bell 2003, 8) and are purportedly silenced. "Narrative domination requires silencing" (Opotow, Ilyes, and Fine 2019, 120). Both hegemonic narratives and counter-narratives are notional. That is, they are typically not literal texts that social actors cite verbatim. And both contain conventional elements, demonstrating that one can only defy convention so much.

Work on hegemonic narratives takes obvious inspiration from the writings of Antonio Gramsci, who identified hegemony, or control through legitimation of the ruling ideas, as a principal instrument of state power under capitalism (Hoare and Smith 1996). The masses consent to the political order: they adopt the logics, including the narratives, that sustain that order as common sense. By definition, common sense requires little explication. Andrews (2004, 1) states: "One of the key functions of master narratives is that they offer people a way of identifying what is assumed to be a normative experience." They contribute, in other words, to the construction of normality. A master narrative can, in Hyvärinen's (2021, 17) view, "exist textually as a system of different versions." Both full-blown, morally reprehensible versions *and* more socially acceptable ones imbued with unsaid, are possible. The morally reprehensible versions receive less use as they provoke objection, by definition. Sandberg (2016) thus observes that many hegemonic narratives are expressed as *tropes,* or abbreviated texts that allude to stories without actually telling them. Tropes depend on the narrator's sense that the interlocutor will know the full story. Again we encounter something unsaid that is presumed to be common knowledge.

To round up this discussion of narrative, hegemony, and counter-hegemony as it pertains to unsaid: "missing" stories include those that are salient within a culture but disseminated tacitly, and those that are stifled insofar as they pose a challenge to elites or the political status quo. These two rather different kinds of "unsaid" stories work in tandem to sustain relations of power and patterns of harm. Beyond identifiable narratives, narrativity may be usefully thought of as one exceptionally effective way of achieving absences.

PLAN OF THE BOOK

The book outlines a set of methods aligned with a qualitative critical discourse analysis.[17] Discourse analysis is a deconstruction of text for meanings. *Critical* discourse analysis undertakes such deconstruction in order to understand relations of power and especially how dominance is sustained. My departure from discourse analysis is that I am specifically and wholly attuned to what has *not* been uttered or recorded instead of what has. The approach treats unsaid things as discursive content. Established points of focus in discourse analysis, including but not limited to figurative expressions, presupposition, and sentence structure, are taken to be potential indications of something unsaid.

The methodology targets two types of harmful not-saying: tacit communication having to do with the exercise of power and infliction of harm, and exclusion of particular subjects. Figure 1 represents these two types in picture form. Table 1 outlines the methods generally.

This introductory chapter has sketched the big ideas that inspired me to develop a method for determining what is unsaid, and specifically where unsaid is serving power. The chapters to follow present

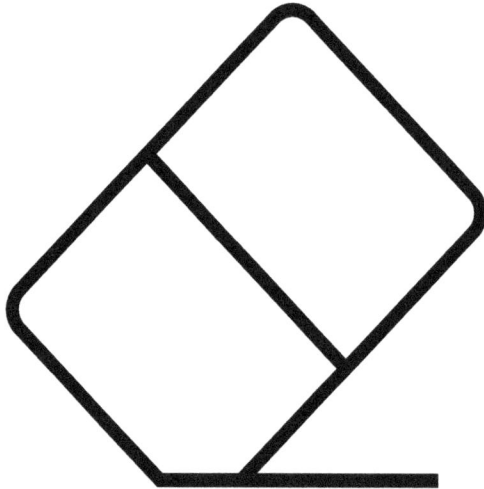

Figure 1. Two types of harmful unsaid. The covered server (*top*) represents concealed messages that contribute to dominance and harm. The pencil eraser (*bottom*) represents exclusion of persons, events, actions, experiences, contexts, and perspectives.

Table 1 Overview of Methods for Unsaid Analysis

Broad focus	Specific foci	Explanation
Patterns of elaboration	Understatement	Saying too little yields unsaid;
	Overstatement	saying too much obscures it.
Figurative expression	Metaphor	Figurative devices say one thing
	Metonymy	and mean another.
Missing subjects	Persons	Persons and things are unjustly
	Events	excluded from texts.
	Actions	
	Experiences	
	Contexts	
	Perspectives	
Social construction of absences	Interlocutors	Unsaid is socially constructed.
	Settings	
	Interdiscursivity	
	Intertextuality	

methods of analysis. The materials I use for exposition in this book are mainly of four kinds: (1) political speech, by which I mean, here, statements issued by politicians *as* politicians as well as statements (e.g., laws or policies) issued by government institutions; (2) a theory of criminal behavior; (3) magazine and newspaper articles on style, beauty, and leisure; and (4) data from interviews with men who perpetrated violence. (On sampling, see the appendix.) My excerpts are brief, intended to demonstrate particular methods of analysis.

The basic strategy is that of discovering two types of unsaid: concealed messages that would expose power-serving purposes and harmful projects; and exclusions whereby persons, events, experiences, contexts, and perspectives go missing.

Chapters 2 through 5 isolate the four main foci of the approach. They set out the logic of inquiry and the tasks that such inquiry entails, which case studies help demonstrate. Chapters 2 and 3 concern concealed messages, or the first type of unsaid. Chapter 4 concerns missing subjects, or the second type of unsaid.

Chapter 2 sets out methods for evaluating too little or too much said. Understatement obviously yields something unsaid, whereas overstatement may bury it under a profusion of words; it may also suppress unspoken tensions and aims. A look at *patterns* of verbosity is useful, as for example when concern about a problem is overstated but one's plans to intervene are hardly mentioned.

Chapter 3 describes the work of probing figurative expression, specifically metaphor and metonymy. The researcher asks what understandings and characterizations of harm, harm's consequences, actors, and targets these rhetorical devices imply.

Chapter 4 outlines the study of missing subjects in texts—that is, the exclusion of persons, events, experiences, contexts, and perspectives. The researcher asks who and what is not in the text but ought to be in terms of impact by the text or in the text. The method explicitly centers harm and justice.

Chapter 5 probes the social dynamism of unsaid more deeply. Taking seriously the social construction of "what" gets communicated, it contemplates the shaping of textual gaps via such influences as proximate interlocutors in concrete settings, cultural structures (e.g., genres), as well as other texts—that is, intertextuality.

Chapter 6 gathers the lessons of the foregoing applications. It also considers thorny issues and potential criticisms: questions of unsaid as having more of a "bright side" than I have allowed; the said as no more determinate than the unsaid; unsaid analysis as less important than material structures; tacit communication as having less of an impact than the explicit kind; or unsaid analysis as instrumental in building conspiracy theories and propaganda. This last chapter reflects on what the methods can and cannot do.

2 Too Little or Too Much Said

Saying too little requires audiences to fill in gaps. Saying too much requires them to figure out what the communicator is getting at amidst the verbosity. The deficits and excesses can be indicators of something meaningful that has gone unsaid (table 2).

My analysis of too little or too much said rests on the field of pragmatics within linguistics as well as an understanding of the cultural conventions of, and sociopolitical contexts for, communication. Linguist H. Paul Grice (1975), whose work was introduced in the previous chapter, advanced a set of conversational maxims, or rules that communicators appear to follow. Three of the Gricean maxims have something to do with *how much* one relays. The "maxim of quantity" states that speakers say what is needed to make their point and not any more. The "maxim of relation" has it that speakers should make relevant contributions. And the "maxim of manner" directs speech to be clear, orderly, and parsimonious. Setting aside Grice's signposts, as an empirical matter, ambiguous speech abounds. Indirectness "is a universal phenomenon" (Thomas 1995, 119) even

---

Table 2   Key Questions for Analyzing Understatement and Overstatement

---

Foci	*Questions*
Understatement	
Not much elaborated	What argumentation, detail, or evidence is the text not supplying?
Silent stakes	What does the communicator stand to gain from the communication, which is not stated?
Ambiguous direction	What action is the text tacitly requesting?
Quiet by comparison	What does the text de-emphasize or fail to mention that is emphasized or discussed elsewhere?
Overstatement	
Excess words	What do the extraneous words and marginal text accomplish?
Regret for the text	What actions by recipients do feeling words enjoin?
Performing engagement	To what extent is discussion of one's concern accompanied by discussion of one's actions?
Intricate characterization	What does detailed, verbose, or highly particular characterization of persons imply?

---

though in being indirect one risks being misunderstood. Actually, being misunderstood, or at least leaving one's meaning vague enough to avoid being accountable for how it is received, may be "the point."

Understatement is more obviously productive of unsaid than is overstatement. Strictly by definition, understatement does not state something. Yet, overstatement obscures understatement and thus often accompanies it. Through overstatement silences are "obscured by words" (Bilmes 1994, 82). Excess text fills the gap that is left when something else is not being said. Thus, whereas this chapter presents understatement and overstatement separately, it is very useful in practice to investigate how they work together—to use a comparative strategy.

To expound the different processes for exposing patterns concerning too little and too much said, the chapter marshals varied examples, mostly drawn from politically relevant speech and a prominent theory in criminology, known as the general theory of crime. These are texts that do or permit harm via unsaid about social problems, that is, issues of some general concern. Patterns of too much versus too little help make unsaid visible.

UNDERSTATEMENT

Understatement may be appreciated for producing something elegant, such as a spare poem or a chic outfit. Less can be more. In this segment of unsaid analysis, less conceals or signals more.

Understatement has a sure place in politics. Leaders say much about positive accomplishments and say little—or nothing—about conditions for which they could be blamed. It is common for leaders to understate the magnitude of problems that would undermine the appearance of mastery or success. For example, in a letter to governors dated March 26, 2020, US president Donald J. Trump wrote of COVID-19, "A number of our fellow citizens have tragically succumbed to its ravages" (*New York Times* 2020). The letter does not give a count of casualties, but instead offers a (metaphoric) summary statement. It is a statement that downplays the impact of COVID-19. By convention, "a number" is surely an inadequate descriptor for the more than 1,300 cumulative deaths in the United States from COVID-19 up to that date (Ritchie et al. 2020).

Where understatement pertains to how the impacts of social problems are enumerated, analysis is fairly straightforward. It may be assessed by asking: Does the wording capture the magnitude of the problem?

Other understatement pertains to the nature or etiology of some problem rather than its impact. The rest of this section on understatement attends to these, and specifically four common kinds of harmful understatement. First, something may be stated but scarcely elaborated. The full import or the logic of the statement is not spelled out. Second, a text may be silent on its stakes: the interests or purposes that it serves are not made clear. Third, and closely related to silence on stakes, a text may be vague about what the communicator is asking for when they seem to be asking for something, which I call ambiguous direction. Fourth, something may be hardly discussed relative to other things, which I call quiet by comparison.

Not Much Elaborated

Communicators may not elaborate because they judge elaboration to be disadvantageous or unnecessary. Elaboration makes the communicator more open to criticism. There is simply more to criticize. Also, the audience will have gained superior judgement from a more complete text, providing a better basis for criticism. To scale back on elaboration is to avoid those possibilities. Or, perhaps innocently, communicators may take the unsaid part to be common knowledge.

Elaborating, and specifically explaining, is tied to power in each of the aforementioned ways. An explanation (or account) is generally expected of subordinates or those deemed deviant. Not explaining is the prerogative of persons and institutions that wield power—consider a retort that is popular among parents, "Because I said so!" Also, dominant logics enjoy presumptive common sense. Dominant and dominating logics have gained a foothold in the present collective consciousness and tend to go unquestioned. By holding back in storytelling, communicators can align the story with master narratives on the surface (Clifton and Van De Mieroop 2016). An example is the report given by a parolee who understates the particulars of interactions with criminalized peers: they maintain some autonomy through selective sharing.

Methodologically, the analyst asks: What statements is the text not elaborating? That is, what additional argumentation, detail, or evidence is the text not supplying? To demonstrate such inquiry, presently I use a case from criminological theory, specifically a theory of the etiology of crime, Gottfredson and Hirschi's so-called general theory. Textual under-elaboration constructs what a criminal is according to the theory, which shapes public policy.

Silent Stakes

Knowing what a communication is designed to achieve is imperative for analyzing understatement. I can understand your cagey way of canceling our lunch date if I know that you wanted to avoid hurting my feelings. But it is not always possible to know others' purposes, precisely because they very often go unstated.

For broad objectives, discourse genre can be a guide. A news article aims to inform, possibly to entertain. An arranged talk with a friend aims to forge personal connection. More specific, though still rather general, purposes may be inferred from context—the section of the newspaper in the first case, a rumor of some interpersonal betrayal in the second case. The question of particular texts, presented and worded as they are, is more complex. What, for example, is the purpose of web pages that meat processing corporations devote to so-called animal welfare (Schally 2018)? Judging from the vast evidence of harm to nonhuman animals and campaigns against such harm, those texts would seem to be discursively accounting for the harm, countering stigma that could undermine consumer favor and ultimately profits. Such reasons for the text form a context that requires some discovery.

In general, as a means of penetrating silence on stakes, the analyst asks: What does the communicator stand to gain from the communication? What could it achieve, and for whom?

Under capitalism, it is easy and usually correct to presume that some statement is tied to the pursuit of financial gain or status; this purpose or stake in communicating can be taken for granted. Theories of intersectional oppression under capitalism point more specifically to preservation of privilege as the purpose of some communication.

Analysis can be quite a bit more nuanced, such as with knowledge of the social contexts for the pursuit of financial gain or professional privilege, including political issues and tensions. Such knowledge helps analysts expose multiple purposes.

Toerien and Jackson's (2019) conversation-analytic study of unsaid in outpatient neurological consultations is illustrative. The authors identify *specific* purposes of an extended exchange between a neurologist and a patient's mother. Broadly, the visit is oriented toward arriving at a medical diagnosis. But the patient's mother is motivated to secure a particular diagnosis of her daughter's condition—that of epilepsy—which the neurologist resists. A *general* purpose is also seen: that of minimizing overt conflict. It is well established that interlocutors typically avoid disputing what the other has said (Goffman 1955; Heritage 1984). They have a stake in saving face—avoiding embarrassment—including for their conversational partner. And so, co-conversationalists tend to disagree in subtle ways, producing unsaid. Conflict avoidance may be considered a background objective that communicators pursue alongside other agendas.

Finally, communicators have a stake in alignment with favored groups and causes. Texts thus commonly put the communicator on the side of "the good," however defined. The notion of alignment is a useful one for silent-stakes inquiry. The analyst might ask whom and what the text appears to be aligning itself with or positively appraising, and then: What might such alignment achieve?

Ambiguous Direction

Closely related to silence on stakes—likewise obscuring purposes—is what I call ambiguous direction. Here, the text is calling for an action that is not explicitly stated. When a teacher announces to students, "It's time to get started," the meaning taken by experienced students is ordinarily: "Put your books away, stop talking, and look at me attentively." That meaning is implicit. What is unsaid is what one seeks to achieve—what action the communicator would wish for.

Indeed, even the fact of an order having been given, in effect, is disguised. How, then, do recipients routinely get the message? They use cultural common sense, embodied as sociolinguistic schemas. Doing so directs them to cooperate or possibly to resist. Resistance can be disobedience, but it cannot be explicit objection to the order, since it was ambiguous in the first place.

With genre-specific exceptions such as poetry and comedy, ambiguity in communication is generally considered suboptimal. "Ambiguity is a fundamental threat to the comprehension process," write Ferreira, Slevc, and Rogers (2005, 264). Ambiguous speech violates Grice's (1975) maxims. However, these ideas and Grice's theory rest on a view of communicative exchange as meant for the exchange of information. In contrast, analysis of silent stakes and ambiguous direction is based on the assumption that utterances serve social purposes—a position famously developed as speech act theory by Austin (1962) and Searle (1969). Some presumed common sense conditions the purposes: for example, depending on the setting, to ask "Are you hungry?" is aptly understood in my culture as an invitation to join me in a meal or accept food that the asker intends to provide. It could also serve as a sly dig, if one's companion is eating a lot or voraciously. Something is communicated *by* communicating less than clearly or fully (Eisenberg 1984). Ambiguity is also a tool for favorable self-presentation. Through ambiguous expression and no other accompanying action, individuals and institutions can achieve certain culturally preferred appearances—for example, of civility, social responsibility, fairness, or objectivity. Soliciting from the other could be obnoxious. Ambiguous direction allows communicators to solicit something while preserving these preferred impressions.

The analyst asks what action the text is requesting. The analyst subsequently investigates the possibility that the request for action, or the action itself, does or supports harm, including a harmful status quo.

An *intention* to conceal something might seem to pertain when a text is silent on stakes or issues an ambiguous directive. Presumably social actors know their own interests and purposes. And yet, certainly they are not always aware of them in the moment of communicating. In any case, the methodology is the same whether social actors know or do not know their interests and purposes, and whether they mindfully hide them or not, although absences of which communicators are unaware may entail more analytical challenges. These, von Münchow (2018, 221) writes, "are rarely identified by recipients or another kind of audience and thus remain to be discovered by the analyst." Unsaid analysis is not tied to the intention to exclude, because impactful exclusions need not be, and often are not, intentional. Indeed, they may not even be perceived by the parties to communication.[1]

The analytical question for discovering ambiguous direction is: What preferred action that is not stated, does the communication point to? As with silent stakes, such action is a matter for interpretation of both wording and the erstwhile purposes and non-purposes of the communicator.

An example of ambiguous direction in text is the kind of verbiage that shrouds an effort to extort, or obtain something through coercion. Ambiguity in that case disguises the coercion.

Early in July of 2019 the US government withheld $391 million in congressionally authorized military aid to Ukraine, crucial to that country's efforts to counter Russian aggression. Later that month, during a phone call on July 25, President Trump pressured Ukrainian president Volodymyr Zelensky to announce a corruption investigation centered on ties between Ukrainian energy company Burisma Holdings and Hunter Biden, son of Trump's political rival Joe Biden. Trump was working from a theory that Joe Biden, when he was vice president, pressured Ukraine to fire its prosecutor general in order to thwart inquiry into possible wrongdoing by Hunter Biden. An announcement of an investigation by Zelensky would perhaps harm Joe Biden, and thus improve Trump's chances of winning a second term in office. Trump's remark to Ukrainian President Volodymyr Zelensky became infamous: "The United States has been very very good to Ukraine. I wouldn't say that it's reciprocal necessarily because things are happening that are not good but the United States has been very very good to Ukraine" (White House 2019).

Trump continued:

> The other thing, there's a lot of talk about Biden's son, that Biden stopped the prosecution and a lot of people want to find out about that so whatever you can do with the Attorney General would be great. Biden went around bragging that he stopped the prosecution so if you can look into it . . . it sounds horrible to me.

Trump assigns himself no place in the formulations "whatever you can do with the Attorney General" and "if you can look into it." He is not a grammatical subject; there is no "I am asking you to look into it," for example. The wording suggests that his counterpart, Zelensky, makes his own choices. It also presents Trump's own interest in the situation as a general moral concern: "It sounds horrible to me." Indeed, Trump is not even among those "talking about" Biden's son or "wanting to find out." He is just a man with an opinion on something, from which he stands apart. Unmotivated as he is, discursively speaking, his part in directing anything is wholly obscured.

The Trump administration and right-wing media observers insisted that the transcript reveals nothing explicit to support allegations of a fraudulent *quid pro quo* or extortion (see e.g. Blake 2019; Re 2019). That defense was satirized by comedian Trevor Noah, whose message was that not-saying is practically the essence of extortion (Wilstein 2019). Reflecting on the Mafia crime family for comparison, Noah commented: "Explicit is the exact opposite of what they do." How to systematically approach the extortive exchange from the perspective of unsaid?

The words "things are happening that are not good" cue the hearer to a problem, as does the negative "I wouldn't say" sandwiched between the repetition of "the United States has been very very good to Ukraine." Trump is asking Ukraine to resolve a relational asymmetry by repairing the things that are "not good." The asymmetry can be expressed as "You have not done enough for us." The "ask" is, "You should do more for us." Trump is alluding to a relationship failure and an obligation.

The key question is: What action is being requested or obliged? To address this question, both fine-grained discourse analysis and analysis of the broad social context are necessary. The analyst asks of each designated text unit (e.g., a sentence) what performance or performances it directs. What should the attentive interlocutor—the person being directed—*do*?

Social context points to *why* the parties to communication would consider the equivocal expression as calling for a particular action. What are the action possibilities known to those parties? What are the things the hearer is in a position to do? The president of Ukraine can launch an inquiry, in the service of "finding out." Social context has a discursive dimension as well, which was discussed above in regard to cultural common sense: it includes what the communicator knows is the taken-for-granted meaning of certain words for certain audiences. President Zelensky of Ukraine would presumably know that to "look into" something entails publicizing such an inquiry, which is Trump's political goal. In another example: "take care of him" stereotypically means committing murder in crime syndicates but does not mean any such thing within families.

Quiet by Comparison

Analysts might also detect understatement concerning a particular topic by comparing the text under study with other texts.[2] The text under analysis does not mention, or makes little of, something that is discussed or even emphasized elsewhere. The latter becomes a reference point.

A first example comes from Alcántara-Plá and Ruiz-Sánchez (2018), who studied migration as "a silenced topic" in political tweets leading up to Spain's 2015 general election. They used news articles in the same time period as a point of comparison for the tweets.

Migration was "a hot topic for the newspapers in 2015" (33), whereas it received far less attention in the space under investigation. The difference suggests ideological investment in the understated text. In another example, Strand (2018) investigated discursive discrimination against sexual minorities by the Ugandan press. Calling the work "cross-media analysis," Strand compared discussion of domestic sexual minorities in two prominent daily newspapers with tweets produced by a sexual-minorities advocacy group. Strand concludes that the newspapers "systematically fail to provide editorially controlled space to LGBTQI individuals or their organizations for self-representation, even when they are directly addressed by others as during the Presidential debate on national TV" (144).

These two studies had analysts comparing coverage of an event or phenomenon in different texts (von Münchow 2018). Analysts can also compare different drafts of a text. Machin and Mayr (2012) studied an Independent Radio News feed against a final broadcast based on the feed, on the matter of the October 2002 bombings in Bali, Indonesia, by militant Islamists, which killed 202 people. They note that "the rewrite has omitted all legal reference," such as terms like "prosecutors" and "defendants," with the result that it "becomes one more story in the war on terror" (39). Machin and Mayr point to the ideological function of the editing, as particular assigned social roles vanish for the sake of telling a familiar story of good versus evil.

One cannot overestimate the methodological value of comparing texts on the attention they devote to different issues or events. The comparison is served by knowledge of the purposes of one media outlet (but not the other), such as a government's investment in maintaining some political status quo. However, the analytic strategy of comparison neglects the possibility that the issue or event under investigation or its context, neglected in *a* text, is also neglected at large: no outlet deems it relevant. In other words, the strategy does not identify broad societal erasures, what I refer to as missing subjects. These are addressed in chapter 4.

Machin and Mayr (2012, 39) describe a strategy for locating voids based on expectations: "We can ask what lexical items are missing that we might expect to be included." Yet, as Partington (2018, 96) points out, looking for "absence when a presence is expected ... raises the question of expected by whom and why." One very good basis for the expectation of presence is research-derived evidence (Venkataraman 2018). An alternative is common knowledge of political, cultural, and linguistic context. Both evidence and common knowledge admit to selection biases. Whatever the basis, researchers should disclose it. They should discuss precisely why they expected something to be included in a text or corpus of texts.

OVERSTATEMENT

With overstatement, words, phrases, paragraphs, sections, and so forth are tangential to some supposedly main point.[3] They do not seem to add anything to the argument or story being crafted, or they do not seem to go with the rest. Within a text, then, the analyst should highlight words, phrases, paragraphs, and sections that add nothing to the text *or* depart from its evidently main point. The key question to ask of seemingly excessive, marginal, or incongruous and perhaps odd text is: What is the excessive text accomplishing? Two ancillary questions are: Does it distract from harm? And is it abetting a potentially harmful course of action? In addition to excess or incongruous verbiage, overstatement may register as regret for the text, performance of engagement, or intricate characterization of individuals in stories.

Excess Words

Common sense about tangents as flawed communication is misguided if the text would distract by design. Excess text, casually known as filler, can help communicators avoid controversial issues or disguise harmful positions. Trump's statement to President Zelensky, discussed above, contains excess wording that obscures the extortionary essence. His "I wouldn't say that it's reciprocal necessarily" is a less direct version of "It is not reciprocal." The extra words circumvent the potentially stronger force of the statement.

Faced with adverse or contentious events, excess words can blunt a message. They can provide cover for an unpopular position. They can also allow communicators to pivot from something they do not want to talk about to something that they do. Excessive words might be seen in a text that conveys two contradictory messages, such as approval and disapproval of something. In that case more ambiguous wording might be used for one message as compared with the other. For example, "Sure, he makes an interesting point, but I still disagree." What exactly is an "interesting" point? "Still disagree" is more straightforward.

Excess wording may pertain beyond particular statements. A whole communicative entity or event can be excessive. Rice (2020) describes "document dumps" in the context of information requests for legal cases, working against understanding: "Tactically, dumping documents is the same as withholding information, since the relevant content is essentially buried under gigantic mountains of other information" (99). Vinitzky-Seroussi and Teeger (2010) describe a performative version of such burying through discursive excess, as the "cacophonous commemoration" of some historic event purposely convened in conjunction with other events—to crowd them out, as it were.

The analyst can search for elements or verbiage that seem unnecessary, strictly speaking, to a main point. These are not central: they are not adding much or anything at all. A common instance of extraneous text, often seen in official responses to challenges to a policy, is a restatement of that policy. The restatement is filler, clearly superfluous since the challenger is already well versed in the policy, hence their challenge.

The analyst can also establish that some wording is excessive by comparing variations in style. The author may tend to use—indeed, the outlet or culture may warrant—a lean or, conversely, a wordy style. So one examines the text for internal departures: the "deviant" text might be excessive. Beyond these leads, it is once again important to share how one makes one's determinations. Determining which words are in excess is a tricky business—a matter of one's culture and socialization, and even a matter of taste.

Critical discourse analysts have considered excess words used to hedge, meaning to "soften the impact of what we have to say, or to mitigate something" (Machin and Mayr 2012, 187). An example of this kind of surfeit of words comes from Nikki Haley, the former ambassador to the United Nations under president Donald J. Trump, during an interview (November 11, 2019) with right-wing commentator Sean Hannity. The interview was meant to publicize Haley's new (2019) book, *With All Due Respect: Defending America with Grit and Grace.* Though at past points critical of Trump, Haley had come to support him, like many Republicans mindful of their political fortunes (Karni and Haberman 2019). In the following excerpt, Haley responds to Hannity's question concerning Trump's call for Ukraine to intervene in the previously discussed alleged misconduct by Joe Biden, Trump's political rival, and Biden's son, Hunter Biden.

> I, in practice, don't think it's good for us to ever ask foreign governments to investigate Americans, but I think it goes to the fact that Americans should be investigating Americans, and Americans should be asking the questions of Joe Biden and asking the questions of his son, and finding out exactly what was going on with that situation and get down to the bottom of it. (Morefield 2019)

In this statement Haley balances criticism of and support for Trump's request. She does so by pivoting very quickly from criticism to support and by including extraneous verbiage such as "in practice." In stipulating "in practice" the text indicates that the expressed disapproval is not absolute.[4] The meaning of "it goes to the fact" may not be precise, but it allows Haley to stage a move from a negative appraisal of Trump to a negative appraisal of the Bidens, and to do so in patriotic terms. Haley's "I . . . don't think it's good" launch to a critique of Trump is a more tepid representation of point of view—it has lower modality—than "the fact" of her critique of the Bidens. The disapproval of Trump's actions is superfluous to where Haley wants to "go" with the statement.

Haley also uses signifiers that tend to inspire feeling—consider her oft-repeated reference to "Americans" within just a short excerpt—but the text is primarily about the need for principled investigation. In contrast, texts can center feeling, and devote space to doing so; we turn next to space filled with expressions of regret.

Regret for the Text

Texts communicate not just propositional content but also affect. Stories convey the feelings (or indifference—lack of feeling) of characters, including feelings that motivated their actions and feelings stirred by the narrated events. Nonfictional texts, such as reports, also indicate feeling-states concerning their content.

In describing content negatively, the speaker/writer may do well to express some measure of regret. Regret for the text potentially creates affiliation between communicator and recipient. If the phenomenon being described is undesirable, the recipient should understand that the communicator is not responsible. The recipient should continue to place trust in the communicator.

An example is an article that appeared in *Marie Claire*, a magazine aimed at women (Thomas 2019), listing the best anti-aging products. It begins:

> In an ideal world, none of us would worry about the visible signs of ageing and would simply be content with the (clichéd) notion of "growing old gracefully." But, sadly, we don't live in an ideal world and when the time comes, most of us will reach for anti-ageing beauty products faster than you can say, well, anti-ageing beauty products. The trouble is the market is flooded with products that claim to do so much.

Here a good many words are used to communicate that the article, and the consumption that it counsels, should not be necessary, but sadly, they are. The overstatement fortifies the notion that the recommended beauty regimen is crucial. Yet, the text seems to acknowledge that the concern to look young has lost at least some of its cultural legitimacy. "Growing old gracefully" is, after all, mentioned as a competing ethos. Change is afoot (Fairclough 1992). A movement for body positivity has become mainstream and, predictably, commodified (Dove.com, n.d.). This article acknowledges the desirability of body positivity and showcases emotional honesty and empathy to frame the felt necessity of products such as it recommends. The analyst examines texts for feeling words and asks what relationships and courses of action these words would enjoin. Might they make harmful practices seem more tolerable, excusable, or inevitable?

Abstract, *orientation*, *preface*, and *paratext* are terms from different academic fields for text that that launches or frames the main text. These are often where the communicator expresses feelings about communicating the very next thing. Hence a parent who "hates to have to" beat a child, or some other authority figure who announces, "I'm sorry, but I am going to have to ask you to leave." This sort of speech before the speech can suggest a position of powerlessness ("have to" and "ask you") while tending to leave actual power in the shadows. A preface might express regret to mark a distinction between the speaker and the character in a presently told *story*. Tim was a research participant who, during a 1999 in-depth research interview with me, recounted having committed sexual violence years before. (I will return to Tim's story across several chapters.) Tim prefaced the story with "I ain't been looking forward to telling you this part of this thing." He gives notice of aversive action but portrays the self as a pleasant and good person all the same, thus fending off condemnation.

Regret for the text can also underscore the unpleasant nature of what will soon be relayed, as when the regretful claim concerns having restrained oneself to this point. "I'm sorry, but I cannot hold back any longer" or "Okay, now I have to say something" signals that the situation is dire, hence the unfortunate diatribe. It says that a serious problem is afoot; it constructs concerns and urges others to recognize them.

Performing Engagement

A special kind of overstatement pertains to texts that reference some social issue or current event about which the public is concerned, but are relatively silent on what is to be done. These texts characteristically say a great deal about concern and values. While they perform engagement, they allow (some) harm to persist uninterrupted. The texts "overstate" concerns and values—amplifying regret—but say little about any other course of action.

A first example of performing engagement hits close to home— the university. The university is a major social institution. A central purpose of (whatever gets called) an institution is to thrive or at least survive. Many contemporary institutions are held to equality and diversity, especially by current and prospective students. At the same time, governing boards, politicians, conservative alumni, and others may not view equality and diversity as priorities or in jeopardy. They may even consider these as preoccupations whose redress itself does harm. Hence university administrators issue statements condemning racism in the face of some racist incident, including incidents beyond the campus, without indicating just what they intend to do (Ahmed 2006).[5]

Universities are certainly not the only performers of engagement. The practice is widespread among institutions generally. This kind of communication serves individuals and groups whenever their goals or values are in conflict with one another or with their practices.

A second example of performing engagement pertains to actions toward nonhuman animals. To understand how industrial-agriculture concerns thwart opposition to the harms they cause to nonhuman animals and the ecological environment, Schally (2018) subjected the website of the multinational corporation Tyson Foods to transitivity analysis (Halliday 1994). Tyson Foods is one of the world's largest processors of chicken, beef, and pork. Transitivity analysis is an approach for deconstructing the discursive representation of action. This method has the analyst clarifying which of six possible types a process may fall into: material, mental, relational, behavioral, verbal, or existential. A review of this framework is in order.

Material processes pertain to acting and have what linguists call a beneficiary: "she hammers a nail." Mental processes pertain to sensing—either cognition, affection, or perception: "I know him," "I like him," or "I hear him." Relational processes pertain to being and having: "she is a teacher," or "she has a job." Behavioral processes pertain to psychological or physical action, with just one sentient party doing the acting: for example, "they watched." Halliday (1994, 107) refers to behavioral processes as on "the borderline between material and mental processes." Verbal processes pertain to saying— "any kind of symbolic exchange of meaning" (140). They characteristically identify the communicator as well as their message and who the message pertains to, as in "The article reported that no one was hurt." Existential processes have to do with existing or happening and are "on the borderline between the relational and the material" (107). Verb forms related to being, happening, and existing are used here, but in contrast to relational processes, only one participant is mentioned: "There was a shooting."

According to Schally (2018), the Tyson Foods website reported engaging in very few material processes concerning the welfare of nonhumans, despite pages with titles like "Environment" and "Animal Well-Being." The "Animal Well-Being" page made pronouncements such as "We've had a corporate office of animal well-being since 2000 and our commitment to responsible stewardship of the animals entrusted to us is part of our company's Core Values— to which all 115,000 of our Team Members subscribe." Schally comments:

Unexamined, the passages from the animal well-being page give the impression that Tyson is proactive and transparent in terms of animal care. On closer inspection, we find that Tyson says a lot about their *belief* in proper animal care and treatment, as evidenced by their disproportionate use of relational and behavioral processes, but very little about what they are actually doing, as evidenced by the absence of material processes. In this way, Tyson is disguising their actions while simultaneously giving the appearance of being forthcoming, by the way the text is constructed. (59)

Tyson builds up who they are, though not what they *do*. Schally's finding of limited material processes where animal well-being is concerned points to a stance on Tyson's part that is "all talk."

Schally's study in effect addresses the business practice known as greenwashing. Defined as the juxtaposition of "poor environmental performance and positive communication about environmental performance" (Delmas and Burbano 2011, 65), greenwashing is a common corporate practice, and it features unsaid. Kangun, Carlson, and Grove (1991) point to three categories of greenwashing in advertisements: use of vague terms, omission of information that could be used to evaluate claims, and false claims. When companies align themselves with environmental organizations and actions without contributing significantly to either, their greenwashing is performance of engagement. Analysis of performance of engagement orients to the question: To what extent is expression of concern accompanied by discussion of actions? Or, using transitivity analysis: To what extent are material processes included among responses to putative concern?

Intricate Characterization

Texts usually, and narrative texts regularly, characterize people and their actions. Such characterizations give a sense of what people are like and what they are not like, what they are inclined to do and what they are not inclined to do. What I have in mind as intricate characterization is a kind of overstatement with very detailed or ver-bose characterization, or a placing of persons into highly particular character positions relative to others. The analysis proceeds from the question: What does intricate characterization of persons imply? The work is similar to that of investigation of excess words, discussed above, except that the focus is on who (different) people are.

My own inclination and experience have me taking a narrative approach to intricate characterization, asking how protagonists, antagonists, helpers, and other characters are portrayed, interac-tively, to make moral points. Consider anti-immigration narratives that cast immigrants as a threat to the nation. When would-be immi-grants are demonstrably sympathetic and vulnerable—for instance, when they are children or asylum-seekers fleeing oppression and other grave hardship—the credibility of the threat characterization is strained (Amnesty International 2018). In that case, the narratives need some tweaking in order to be broadly accepted. One possible adjustment is to characterize migrants as victims led astray or exploited by threatening others or elements. Thus condemnation is deflected (Loseke 2007, 86), and innocence is weaponized. To ration-alize the criminalization and possible mistreatment of such victims, the narrative of victimization must be nuanced. Overstatement can help. An article by David Marcus in the conservative online outlet *The Federalist* (November 25, 2019) is illustrative, including this excerpt:

> So when frustrated migrants, perhaps emboldened by irresponsible rhetoric from the American left, simply try to force their way in, how ought our country respond? It seems fairly obvious that the correct response is the one they met: a forceful one. The right response ensures that our border is secure and cannot be infiltrated by anyone who decides to storm it, throw rocks, and run into America.

This text directs audiences to accept an anti-immigration response that is "forceful" and necessarily so.

Using adjectives, adverbs, and verbs, presumably judiciously cho-sen, the text casts as foes both migrants and the American left, even as these are differently positioned moral characters. Migrants are afforded a reason for their bad behavior—they are "frustrated"— whereas the American left is not. Actions in the text are: "try to force their way in," "decides to storm," "throw rocks," and "run into America." The qualifier "simply" constructs these actions as careless. The actors are irresponsible, not desperate. "Anyone" cues the random, pervasive nature of the action, qualities that construct dangerousness all the more for being starkly nonspecific.

Intricate characterization of who one is, how one feels, and what one favors does self-positioning and boundary-drawing work, even in texts not immediately discernible as a story. For her master's thesis, my student Sam McIntyre examined official communications from corporations touting their meatless food products. One text in her corpus is a website statement from the Kellogg's company, whose MorningStar Farms division produces meatless foods:

> Seems like everywhere we turn right now, people are talking about plant-based-this and plant-protein-that. And we couldn't be happier. See, we've been making and innovating better-for-you, better-for-the-planet veggie foods since the very beginning. Over 40 years of spreading plant-based love through everyday food for everyday folks. No futuristic franken-food or all-or-nothing activism. Just uncompromisingly delicious vegetarian and plant protein takes on America's favorite foods, for every appetite and every part of the day. That's why we continually produce some of America's most-loved and most eaten plant-based foods. Burgers to bacon, pulled pork to corn dogs, vegetarian to vegan; MorningStar Farms is plant-based goodness made for everyone. (Kellogg's, n.d.)

McIntyre was struck by the folksy, conversational style and tone of the statement, with its colloquialisms ("plant-based-this and plant-protein-that," "everyday folks"), sentence fragments ("Over 40 years"), and cheery affect ("we couldn't be happier"). With strong narrativity ("we've been making . . . since the beginning"), the text casts the company ("we") as a happy partner to "America." Overall the text is pleasant, though disparaging of "futuristic franken-food" and "all-or-nothing activism." Its populism is friendly on the surface ("made for everyone") but also somewhat coded through its critique of science and social activism. It extends the comforting reassurance that the company has been doing much the same thing for a long time. All that has changed is that "people are talking." Thus the company aligns itself with that swath of the public that is not only not vegan or vegetarian but suspicious of these as progressive and elite identities that threaten fundamental change.

MorningStar/Kellogg's faces an interesting challenge. They want to grow their market share. Ostensibly they would do so by reaching persons who are not already consuming meatless products, but this group may be considered to include those with negative preconceptions about vegans and veganism. Furthermore, like other corporations that market both meat and meatless products (e.g., Gardein/ ConAgra and Raised and Rooted/Tyson Foods), MorningStar/ Kellogg's is incentivized not to "cannibalize" their own stalwart line of meat products. They must tout the new, non-meat item but not encourage their meat consumers to purchase it in lieu of meat. It would do neither to show meat in a negative light nor to argue explicitly against non-meat diets.

CASE STUDY: UNDERSTATEMENT AND OVERSTATEMENT IN A THEORY OF CRIME

From particular kinds of overstatement, I turn now to a case study of how understatement and overstatement may be discerned in a text. Harm-sustaining patterns of verbosity can be detected in the theory set out by Michael Gottfredson and Travis Hirschi in their much-cited 1990 book, *A General Theory of Crime*. This case shines a light on the value of a comparative approach, which assesses patterns of both understatement and overstatement, rather than either alone: the object of interest is "nonuniform patterns of elaboration" (Presser 2019, 417).

Like many other theories of crime, Gottfredson and Hirschi's theory directs attention to antisocial tendencies individuals possess. The authors maintain that the tendency to commit crime and other antisocial behavior is a manifestation of low self-control, which stems from neglectful parenting. "In order to teach the child self-control, someone must (1) monitor the child's behavior; (2) recognize deviant behavior when it occurs; and (3) punish such behavior" (97). In the story of antisociality that the authors tell,[6] parental neglect of any one of those three tasks is the main event. The antisocial propensity becomes an enduring trait once early childhood is reached. Persons "who lack self-control will tend to be impulsive, insensitive, physical, risk-taking, short sighted, and nonverbal, and they will tend therefore to engage in criminal and analogous acts" (179), depending on opportunities.

The general theory of crime supports penal and other social harm. It does so by centering crime-proneness in individuals rather than social practices and thus promoting carcerality, by obscuring the role of the state and public policies in producing "crime," by minimizing the extent of harm-doing by the organized and the powerful, and by reinforcing the vilification of overtaxed, unsupported caregivers, who are disproportionately marginalized women, with ultimate impacts on support for social programs and entitlements. Remarkably for having crafted a theory that assigns criminogenesis almost exclusively to parenting, the theorists take no clear position on programs and policies to help parents parent. The main target of any policy deducible from their theory should be "child-rearing practices" (274), and yet they also state: "All that is required to activate the system is affection for or investment in the child" (97). That is, the minimally concerned parent will do an adequate job of teaching self-control. "Affection for or investment in" one's children are matters of attitude. Public assistance could not help the challenged individual, because the problem is their own indifference and indolence.

That message is familiar. The idea that "all that is required" is the right attitude is consistent with cynical, censorious, neoliberal, and racist attitudes on social supports for the less-well-off in the United States. It is consistent with the uniquely American and broadly consequential story that holds that normal people do not need other people (Polanyi 1989) and that "needy" people are taking advantage of other people (Wacquant 2009). Not coincidentally, these others are cast as a wellspring of criminality. In any number of conservative commentaries on public resources, the potential beneficiaries are represented as lazy and fraudulent. They are inclined to squander assistance instead of using it to achieve autonomy, which is the valorized state. They have too many children—the better to take advantage of public resources—while not caring much for any one child. Black people are especially likely to be cast in these ways. Lurking here, too, is the idea that women's love should trump all kinds of obstacles to keeping family well and together. That idea again bars from consideration features of structure, including adequate income. Gottfredson and Hirschi reproduce these discourses, though with a rather light touch. They do not dwell on parental attitude, even less on the general matter of what shapes childrearing practices.

A General Theory of Crime foregrounds issues the authors have with criminology. Thus the book's preface begins: "We have for some time been unhappy with the ability of academic criminology to provide believable explanations of criminal behavior" (xiii). The first chapter likewise launches by remarking on what disappoints them about criminology. To put the matter in narratological terms, the chief adversaries in the main story of *A General Theory of Crime* are other criminologists. Prefacing the story that Gottfredson and Hirschi tell of the coming-into-being of offenders, is their story of themselves as knowing doubters in the world of academic criminology. It is a factional story, to which the story of antisociality is put across as secondary.

Gottfredson and Hirschi's privileging of that factional story helps us make sense of their understatement of theoretical propositions. They are generally silent on the sources they deploy for their theoretical propositions, or even their empirical logic. They offer no explanation as to why caretaker affection and investment are "all that is required" for things to go right for maturing humans (97). Developmental psychology could help here but is not reckoned with. The authors are candid in calling their claim that crime syndicates are usually short-lived (hence their existence does not undermine the theory) "a good guess" (213). Yet they provide no research support for their guess—nor any indication of why it is good. In general, they present propositions about crime and its perpetrators as facts that require neither qualification nor empirical evidence (e.g., "crimes are not a good source of stable income," 164). At the same time, the text neglects to include the voices or even to discuss the actual life experiences of those designated as antisocial, or their culpable caregivers, or their victims. These subjects are missing, a matter I return to in chapter 4. The conflict with other criminologists is evidently of greater concern to them than is their theorization of crime.

Gottfredson and Hirschi define crime as "acts of force or fraud undertaken in pursuit of self-interest" (15) without any consideration of how force and fraud get construed by state practitioners.[7] Very many crimes—not to mention legal practices that cause harm—appear neither in the authors' elaboration of what crime is nor in the crime statistics they provide. Such omissions are par for the course for criminology and criminal justice broadly (Websdale and Ferrell 1999), but these omissions are especially striking. An example is seen in their delineation of the two "basic varieties" of homicide. One variety is instigated when "people who are known to one another argue over some trivial matter" (Gottfredson and Hirschi 1990, 33). The other variety is an unplanned killing during the execution of some other crime. The basis for these two basic varieties is unstated. Concerning the former variety, the qualifier of "trivial" seems to strongly warrant explication, as available data, including interviews with survivors of intimate partner violence, suggest that the "trivial matter" typically centers on the woman's autonomy and faithfulness. In general, both varieties, and thus the theorists' codification of

homicide, omit all kinds of killings, both legal and illegal, and especially killings of highly vulnerable persons.

Their perspective on harm is institutional. It cleaves to state designations. For example, they seem unconcerned about harm per se
when they offer the following in support of their claim that most
rapes are between strangers: "Family members and close friends
apparently rarely jeopardize long-term relations by *committing or
reporting* rape" (36; emphasis mine). Here unreported rape does not
count as rape. On that basis the authors conclude that rape within
interpersonal relationships or on a date is rare. In this way they minimize various forms of harm and reify the state as arbiter of harm.

It is easy to overlook the authors' silences—and even to come
away with a sense of abundant argumentation—given the verbosity
of the book. In the space of 275 pages, the authors offer protracted
discussions of the history of criminological thought, the nature of
crime, types and correlates of crime and how the general theory
makes sense of them, and how the theory ought to be tested.
Gottfredson and Hirschi set out numerous critiques: they "disavow"
much (4). They critique various criminological approaches, particularly what they call positivistic theories. They pan concerns about
age-graded patterns of offending. They disparage arguments that so-
called white-collar crime differs from so-called conventional crime.
They are critical of criminologists' putative failure to articulate the
essential nature of crime.[8]

In view of their strong critique of current theoretical understandings of crime, it comes as no surprise that Gottfredson and Hirschi
are also critical of current strategies of crime reduction. After all,
anti-crime strategies are informed by some sort of understanding of
crime. They spend nearly seven pages of the book censuring selective
incapacitation, a strategy of crime control that seeks to isolate—to
remove from general circulation—high-risk persons. They are
opposed to jail and other "short-term institutional experiences"
(232). The analyst, taking stock of these many critiques, should ask
what Gottfredson and Hirschi are *not* critical of. They are not critical

of criminal justice. They are silent on both general incapacitation and *long-term* institutionalization—the policies that we have actually implemented in the United States (Mauer 2006; Travis, Western, and Redburn 2014). Thus, they do not take issue with carceral control. They are tacit supporters of that status quo.

I find notable excessive wording in the preface to *A General Theory of Crime*, where the authors declare that they "see little hope for important reductions in crime through modification of the criminal justice system" (xvi). The surplus phrasing, "modification of," is peculiar. It tempers the authors' disapproval: something about criminal justice practices frustrates them, but the practices are not altogether ill-conceived. In fact, the general theory unmistakably points to the futility of *any* intervention in adulthood, because it holds that criminality is an established tendency after childhood: socialization of the child "appears to be largely irreversible" (107). One would therefore expect the theorists to judge as useless criminal justice practices in general, including those currently in effect. In the abstract, "modification of" (the criminal justice system) is ambiguous. It indicates change from what is, and therefore can mean more *or* less criminal justice. The context of the statement was the late 1980s (when the authors were in all likelihood writing), which saw a historic peak in the incarceration rate in the United States (Travis, Western, and Redburn 2014, 34). Gottfredson and Hirschi are saying we should not divert from that punitive course, but saying it ambiguously.

Let me review what I did methodologically with this case, and what I suggest as a viable process for analyzing understatement and overstatement. I asked three overarching questions: What does there seem to be too much of? What does there seem to be too little of? And what are these patterns doing for the logic of the text? I approached the text in terms of (1) specific wording and (2) discussion, thereby tracking fine-grained textual exploration and logical development, respectively. Of wording, I asked: What wording is excessive? Are any words extraneous? What words are scant or absent? Of discussion, I asked: What points are made in excess?

Table 3   Outline of Analysis of Understatement and Overstatement

Steps	Illustration (Gottfredson and Hirschi 1990)
Examine wording	
Scant wording	*some trivial matter*
Excess words	*modification of the criminal justice system*
Examine discussion	
Scant discussion	Perspective of parents
	Research grounds for various theoretical propositions
	Various forms of harm
Excessive discussion	Inadequacy and blunders of criminological theory

What discussions are scant or absent? Of the various resulting findings, I asked: What are these overstatements and understatements doing? That is, what logics are they contributing to? What tensions are they obscuring? Most of the unsaid and therefore most of my unsaid analysis of *A General Theory of Crime* pertained to the level of discussion rather than wording (table 3).

The several criticisms in Gottfredson and Hirschi's book directed me to track what they took issue with and what they did not. An important point for methodology is that analytical moves may come into view in ways specific to the text at hand. I discerned too much wrong with criminological theory and too little wrong with criminal justice.

CHAPTER SUMMARY

This chapter has considered patterns of understatement and overstatement that generate impact through unsaid. Understatement is the more obvious source of unsaid. It admits to some variation that analysts can search for—such as by considering whether there was more that should have been elaborated. Overstatement operates as camouflage and subterfuge. It is an aspect of hedging, such as between two contrary positions. It may act as a verbal bridge to that which the communicator would like to dwell on.

Understatement related to power and harm is seen when not much is elaborated and when the text is silent on stakes or delivers ambiguous direction. A text may fail to provide specifics or examples of assertions, or grounding assumptions or evidence. *Silent stakes* and *ambiguous direction* are my terms for texts that only tacitly convey their own purposes and functions. Speech act theory provides a foundation for these twin concepts, by demonstrating that speech does things. In other words, all speech has functions, beyond informing. The functions of present concern are concealed, and they are consequential to some harm. It bears repeating that unsaid analysis does not presume that communicators are aware of their own purposes in communicating. The guiding question for inquiry into understatement is: Has enough been explained or disclosed for adequate understanding?

Overstatement includes excess words, regret for the text, performance of engagement, and intricate characterization. Excess words can provide cover to an ideological position seemingly at odds with the rest of the communication. They may hedge, that is, mitigate the impact of a core statement. Regret for the text can minimize the communicator's complicity in a harmful practice or situation by framing it as inescapable. The subtext is that the communicator plays no active role in the harm. Overstatement to convey regret for the text facilitates the social production of innocence in the present. Characterologically, it sets the affective tone for the text and colors the communicator empathic. Intricate characterization overstates with its constructions of who characters are, through various parts of speech (e.g., adjectives and verbs). An apparent excess of descriptors for a person or group may disguise justification for harming them. The guiding questions for inquiry into overstatement generally are: Is some text extraneous? And if so, what is the extraneous text accomplishing? Determinations of what is extraneous will depend on close reading. It is also facilitated by the analyst's prior knowledge of whatever the text is about.

Analysis of understatement and overstatement is best conceived as a joint exercise, as in the case study of Gottfredson and Hirschi's so-called general theory of crime. Patterns of elaboration—too much or too little—were investigated in tandem. My background knowledge in criminology and sociology facilitated my analysis of that prominent theory of crime. Much criticized for tautological reasoning, the theory and its devastating logic—parenting under constraint is reconceived as failure now and for the next generation—rely upon myriad silences, shrouded by a prolonged and preeminent recounting of the authors' struggle against the rest of criminology. Thus do the theorists bury their support for systems of oppression.

I empathize with Gottfredson and Hirschi. Some of my own past writing—and probably more than I am now able to grasp—lends support, though stealthily, to systems of oppression. For example, I have used the word "offenders" in referring to imprisoned people (Van Voorhis and Presser 2003), thus reading "criminality" off of the situation of imprisonment. "Offender" is a kind of synecdoche built on a master status: offending occludes all other action, then becomes shorthand for the actor. It is a figurative expression tied to a massive, profitable, harmful system. My wish to develop a methodology for identifying unsaid is in part motivated by the recognition that I have been a heedless conveyor of cultural logics, including harmful ones, and a wish to avoid that role in the future as much as I can.

The next chapter investigates figurative expression, which uses words that diverge from their supposedly literal meanings to say without saying. Like overstatement, figurative expression is a manifest presence that can cloak important absences.

3 Figurative Expression

On hearing that someone is a "pig," one is supposed to understand that the individual is not actually that animal. To say that someone is a "pig" in the US context is to imply, but not say, that the individual is messy, gluttonous, or otherwise offensive. The label is figurative. Figurative communication is generally defined as nonliteral communication. When used figuratively, words are not supposed to be understood in terms of their technical or official meaning such as is found in most dictionaries.

Shifty by reputation, figurative expression can nonetheless represent lived reality better than anything else, within particular cultural contexts. Saying that I love my children "deeply" seems to allow a more precise, evocative rendering of that love than I could accomplish with a descriptor like "very much" or even "tremendously." "Deeply" conjures the *feeling* of my love. Long-serving figurative expressions tend to be immediately understood, and as Goatly (2007, 22) points out, "there is a case for saying that literal language is simply conventionalised metaphor." Giora (1999) presents research evidence that people actually bypass, cognitively, the literal meaning of an expression if the figurative analogue is "salient"—conventional, familiar, or frequently heard. If figurative communication is sometimes truer and taken up at least as readily as literal communication, then figuration should not be maligned on the grounds of efficacy. It may be doing unrivalled work in terms of comprehension and communication.

And yet, figurative communication does accomplish a kind of sleight of hand, for it borrows significance discriminatingly. It takes some aspects of, say, "pig" or "deeply" and leaves the rest. As Fludernik (1996, 90) neatly puts it: "Not all attributes of a rose can be fruitfully applied to one's beloved: she has no thorns, does not need to be watered daily, nor does she grow in flowerbeds or on hedges." The attributes that pertain in the application to a loved one—the beauty and delicateness of roses—are supposedly cultural common knowledge. Such common knowledge goes unsaid. The figurative slur—the person as pig—provokes not because it is novel but because it is widely accepted for its rudeness. Thus, figurative speech imports extratextual, shared meaning—in the case of insult, that the one being denigrated is a nonhuman, a less-than creature, and furthermore foul. These qualities are not spelled out but are nonetheless brought to bear.

This chapter considers figuration as facilitating important harm-promoting omissions and thus as another productive focus of unsaid analysis. The analytical approach is centered on metaphor and metonymy, both of which involve substitutions and thus casting something aside. As Fuery (1995, 168) observes: "Both metaphor and metonymy operate on a level of absence—the former as absence and replacement, the latter as absence and remainder."[1] The empirical examples for demonstrating analysis are texts concerning public policy and interpersonal violence.

METAPHOR

A metaphor refers to one phenomenon in terms of a qualitatively different one. The metaphors of the world are numerous. Love as deep, human being as pig, and beloved as a rose have already been discussed, in the short space of the foregoing introduction to this chapter.

Strategic communicators use metaphors to imply things, including forbidden or harm-promoting things, without saying them. Earlier times in the West brought a range of popular songs (e.g., the Beatles' song "Drive My Car") having sexual relations as their unmentioned topic. The metaphor cloaks the "actual" meaning because communicating it verbatim would presumably be sanctioned. In art, a dodge such as this is purposely provocative: the song is transgressive and gets away with it. Yet, metaphor need not be deliberately or even knowingly deployed. Metaphors are deeply ingrained within our language and collective cognition. This more profound aspect of metaphor is highly significant sociologically, because metaphor can help institutions and people disguise abuse and/or avoid contemplating abuses, with the effect of maintaining power. Thus, for example, the logic of human dominion over nonhumans, which does massive harm in the world, has penetrated common ways of speaking about social life and, while speaking, being understood. It is entirely conventional, but not innocent, to insult humans by calling them animals. In speaking this way we reinforce a hostile stance toward animals. Hence metaphors leave two kinds of things unsaid: the literal wording that the metaphor supplants, and unstated aspects of the source domain, or the realm of experience from which the metaphor draws.

Metaphoric Thought

Various experts on metaphor point to its broad relevance to human experience and action, including power and the abuse of power.

They emphasize the cognitive, and not simply the linguistic, nature of metaphor. Preeminent among them, Lakoff and Johnson (2003) refer to "metaphorical thought" as "unavoidable, ubiquitous, and mostly unconscious" (272). They cast doubt on the very idea of literal or metaphor-free expression.

It is challenging to think and speak differently about the stuff of the world than as it has already been linguistically constructed for us, and metaphors have a big part to play in said constructions. Machin and Mayr (2012, 165) observe that "when metaphors become the dominant way of thinking about a phenomenon it may become very difficult to challenge the metaphors used to describe it, since these become the commonsense or naturalised way of understanding the world." For "the particular language we speak predisposes us to think and act in certain ways" (Goatly 2007, 24). Metaphors and other figurative devices create a particular sort of byway for cognition. We think in *their* terms.

Enter hegemony. Metaphoric thinking can do the bidding of established social arrangements. Consider the commonplace formulation that one is "spending time" with one's family. The logic is economic (Messner and Rosenfeld 2012). It reflects the capitalist economic frame that commodifies experience, with family time being another item on the deficit side of one's budget. The unsaid, as Goatly (2007, 100) points out, is that the "time spent" is not an end in itself, because "things which we do as an end in themselves do not need to be brought within utilitarian calculation and commodified." I may resent my family for "taking" my time—a valuable holding in my portfolio. Or I may feel that the time spent is "valuable." Favorable or unfavorable as I may regard it, being with my family is conceived in terms that align with a particular political economy. Through language, the political economy has, in effect, annexed cognition.

When we are conceiving of something in one way, we are not conceiving it in another way. As such, metaphor directs us to not think and to not say various things. Analysts can therefore ask not just what the metaphor is saying in a particular utterance but also what thought and communication it is supplanting or inhibiting.

Metaphor Domain Analysis

The central question I want to ask of metaphors, for unsaid analysis, is: What reality do they gesture to without putting it into words?[2] The distinction that Lakoff (1993) draws between source domain and target domain is useful for addressing this question. Metaphors, again, draw connections between one experiential domain and another. Lakoff refers to metaphor as "a mapping across conceptual domains" which "sanctions the use of source domain language and inference patterns for target domain concepts" (208). For example, in a reference to "waves of immigration," *wave* is an entity from the source domain of natural phenomena (e.g., oceans), and *immigration* is the target domain. The particulars of each domain that inspire and ground the correspondence are not usually elaborated. Some specifics of the source domain are irrelevant. I trust that reasonable readers will grasp that the watery and wet qualities of waves have no relevance when one is referring to "waves of immigration." Rather, the phrase connotes something overwhelming, uncontrollable, and potentially deadly, *like* the waves of an ocean (van Dijk 2018, 242). The source domain "brings" the significance and does so without being blatantly derogatory or coming out with a definite position.

For conducting a metaphor domain analysis I recommend a four-step process. First, the analyst develops an inventory of the metaphors in the material chosen for study. This step can be challenging. Figuration is so thoroughly integrated into our communication that it can be hard to identify many, and much less all, instances: the expression does not strike us as rhetorical. Consultation with databases of metaphors can be useful in this regard.[3] The second step is to cull from the list those metaphors that might be theoretically relevant: they have the potential to address questions of interest. For example, guided by critical perspectives on power, the analyst would mark out metaphors that have anything to do with agency. The third step is to place the target and source domains side by side. The fourth and final step is to query the source and target domains. The analyst brings common knowledge as well, as I nominate the following three questions for the query:

- What are things like in the source domain?[4]
- What are things like in the target domain?
- What is being implied about the target domain? That is, what is not said?

Two samples of text, pertaining to rape and to governmental responses to COVID-19, respectively, give a basic demonstration of the method. The former is a transcribed research interview. The latter is a letter from president Donald J. Trump to state governors. Said and unsaid in these cases come from a regular person and a powerful politician, respectively, but both have ramifications for patterns of harm.

Case Study: "I Coulda Honored That" and Other Metaphors in a Story of Rape

In the spring of 1999, for a research project on the storied identities of men who had perpetrated violence, I conducted four separate interviews with a man I called Tim.[5] During the second interview, which took place April 19, 1999, Tim recounted having sexually assaulted a 17-year-old girl in 1977, when he was 26.[6] The victim was babysitting the children of an acquaintance of his. After bar-hopping and intent on more drinking at the home of one woman he had met while out, Tim talked his way into her home with another man. Consecutively, both men raped the teenager.

In telling the story of raping Tim used many metaphors, as one does in recounting any story. These metaphors helped construct Tim as a basically decent person (Presser 2008). My question here is: What is unsaid but communicated through metaphor?

The story began with a meta-discursive introduction: "I ain't been looking forward to telling you this part of this thing."[7] (This introduction was last discussed in chapter 2, in terms of the sort of over-statement I called regret for the text.) Thus, Tim expressed shame and concern for my possible disapproval. Here I will step away from ethnographic observations, including reflections on the connection that Tim and I forged, and instead illuminate how "this part" and other metaphors communicated unsaid things.

By figuring the assault as a "part" Tim detaches that violation from the rest of his life. The metaphor of life as a physical whole and life events as parts allows him to communicate tacitly that the whole episode was out of character. To call an episode of life a "part" is rather conventional. All manner of linguistic disaggregation of "a life" has us separating out past selves (e.g., by episode or by year), usually for innocent reasons. Tim would also use other metaphors to imply that his violent conduct—which also included aggravated assault and attempted murder—was atypical of him even as he had done a fair amount of it. I will focus on the only instance of sexual violence he told me about, and the ways in which metaphors communicated meanings he made of that violence—and of himself and his victim—without fully explicating those meanings.

Tim figuratively used words and phrases that emphasize his agency *and* lack of agency relative to his own body and the victim. That is, in the story world he wields proper authority over the victim at the same time that he is not acting of his own volition but physically constrained by what the victim does. In the lengthy excerpt that follows, I put the metaphors I wish to highlight in bold. For expository purposes, table 4 highlights the same selection of metaphors that Tim used.

An', the next thing I know, we were kissin' an' stuff, an' **one thing led** to another an' we—we were fondling each other—and everything was real consensual! An' uh, an' she—you know just—as it went on a little bit further . . . an' then she just got up and said, I changed my mind. I don't want to do this. My boyfriend might found [*sic*] out. A—It **just freaked me out**—I—ya kn—I—**just freaked me out**—I was just sorta **stunned** there for a minute. I didn't know anything about her boyfriend. An' uh—I just—I don't know—I just sort of—I started gettin' mad about it.

Table 4   Illustrating Metaphor Domain Analysis

Steps	Illustration ("Tim")
Develop an inventory of metaphors in the text	*one thing led*
	freaked me out
	stunned
	honored
	bring everything so close
	finished
	playin' an intimidation game
Identify metaphors of interest from the inventory	*stunned*
	honored
	finished
Place source and target domains side by side	*stunned*
	SOURCE: physical attack
	TARGET: emotional reaction
Ask questions:	
What are things like in the source domain?	Corporal, incapacitating
What are things like in the target domain?	Emotional
What is being implied about the target domain?	Tim is powerless over his reaction

---

I mean, you know, if—you know, 10 minutes before that, I **coulda honored that.** You know, I just felt I **coulda honored that.** I—I ain't got no problem with a girl saying now—you know?—you know—I still don't. But I—I just got pissed. I mean, I—just—to go that far, and **bring everything so close,** an' then say no, I just. I told her, I said you gotta **finish** this. You gotta finish this. This ain't right. That you finish this! An' she didn't want to do it. An' I just got mad. Said, well you'll finish it. I just told her you'll finish it. An' uh, instead of finishing it orally,—I had—I just made her lay down on the couch. It's not that I forced her on the couch. I just told her to lay—I said you lay down. I—I was **playin' an intimidation game.** I didn't lay a hand on her. I was just intimidation—usin' my voice an' tryin' to sound threatening.

The text amply indicates powerlessness through the idioms "the next thing I know" and "one thing led to another." When the victim expressed her wish to withdraw from the encounter, Tim was "just sorta stunned." To be stunned is to be rendered unconscious, or bodily incapacitated. The source domain for "stunned" is physical force rendering someone unconscious.

Actually, Tim constructs himself as passive in a few ways. Tim conjures sex as a project (Beneke 1982) that the victim manages. She can "finish" sex but refuses to. What does it mean to "finish" sex? By patriarchal convention, it is marked by orgasm, and specifically male orgasm. That male orgasm marks the conclusion of sexual activity is unsaid and culturally pervasive. The sought-after achievement is male pleasure. To "finish" sex points to the victim's power in the situation.

Whereas Tim conjures himself as passive in relation to his body and in relation to the victim, he is also the authority figure within the sexual interaction. The counterfactual "I coulda honored that" (the victim's changing her mind) is highly suggestive of that assumed position of authority. Contracts are honored; so are requests. One also honors one's ancestors or principles, though these meanings do not seem to apply because of the object of "honored" in Tim's remark, which is "that." He is referencing the victim's desire, her entreaty. The victim had no actual contract and was not obviously making a request. "Honored" here is not literal. Yet, Tim has in effect rendered her statements to the effect of wanting to stop as a *request*. Lacking power, one does not "honor" requests; rather, one makes them and hopes they will be accepted. In contrast, the one who "honors" wields power. Tim is in charge, though he claims that role with no small amount of hedging (e.g., "I just felt I coulda").

Power paradox is my expression for the conjunction of claims of agency and claims of lack of agency (Presser 2013). I have argued that a discursive power paradox is conducive to harm-doing. The pairing of "logics of license and powerlessness" (47) works to legitimize and inspire harm toward a reduced target. Why? First, the pairing creates, in rather overdetermined fashion, the discursive conditions for moral absolution. Second, depending on the story in which the power paradox appears, the pairing may also create the emotional arousal that compels a kind of leaning into the transgressive action. The present inquiry shows that the logics of license and powerlessness may be communicated rhetorically and moreover implicitly.

Case Study: The War on COVID-19

Formal communications, including government statements and scientific theories—no less than remarks made and stories told by regular people—are replete with metaphors. These metaphors can be extremely consequential. In a published letter from then US president Donald J. Trump to state governors in March 2020, we can see the use of metaphor and how it does significant political work. The metaphor I will focus on constructs social intervention as war.

War is a metaphor that gets used quite variously, especially by politicians. It has promoted harm, and it has galvanized opposition to harm. As discourse analysis and pragmatics show generally, the discursive context, and not just a particular word or expression, is important. The case of the war on COVID-19 highlights the role of discursive context in weaponizing unsaid.

Coronavirus disease 2019 (COVID-19) first came to widespread notice in late December 2019 in Wuhan, China. On March 11, 2020, the World Health Organisation declared the coronavirus outbreak a global pandemic. Government measures to mitigate the rapid spread of COVID-19 included border closings, compulsory or recommended social distancing and protective face masks, and school, work, and other business shutdowns. Financial support for citizens, businesses, and whole economies suffering due to the pandemic were also a major focus of governmental action. Whereas the precise impact of the various interventions may not be measurable, there is ample evidence that shutdowns and social distancing saved many lives and that earlier restrictions would have saved far more (Achenbach 2020; Jewell and Jewell 2020; *Lancet* 2020).

Yet, denial of the magnitude and even the veracity of the crisis—by political leaders, community leaders, media figures, and other individuals—was and still is (as of this writing) common.[8] Peak infection and death rates from COVID-19 in the United States were still far off when president Donald J. Trump tweeted, on March 23, 2020, "We cannot let the cure be worse than the problem itself" (Blake 2020). Trump would soon encourage resistance to states' social distancing orders. His express concern was with the national economy, and, critics noted, his own political and economic fortunes. During a live Fox News "town hall" broadcast on March 24, Trump said: "You can destroy a country this way, by closing it down" (Reuters 2020). However plain Trump's concern for the economy was, he would still do well to understate it, simply because indifference to human life is widely considered depraved. Hence Trump's claims that economic ruin would cause people despair, with potential outcomes such as suicide (Olson 2020). "Staying at home," he said, "leads to a different kind of death" (Cathey and Arnholz 2020). Trump praised as "warriors" both front-line health workers *and* ordinary Americans who would forego social distancing for the sake of reopening the economy (Oprysko 2020).

On March 26, President Trump sent a letter to governors stating his intention to issue new, more flexible social distancing guidelines. One paragraph of the letter reads: "With each passing day, our increasingly extensive testing capabilities are giving us a better understanding of the virus and its path. As testing gives us more information about who has been infected, we are tracking the virus and isolating it to prevent further spread. This new information will drive the next phase in our war against this invisible enemy" (*New York Times* 2020).

The metaphor of war is quite explicit ("war against this invisible enemy"). Before I unpack the metaphor in this text, I wish to discuss its use in political speech generally.

War rhetoric was a commonplace for Trump, as it is for political leaders generally, authoritarian (Fuchs 2019) and other (Blumenthal 2020). Presidents Richard Nixon and Ronald Reagan famously waged "wars" on drugs. War rhetoric by politicians, taking the form of us-versus-them, good-versus-evil binary codes and apocalyptic stories (Barrera 2017; Smith 2005), is demonstrably consequential (Whitford and Yates 2003). War metaphors have nurtured ineffective, wasteful, and ultimately lethal action patterns, as journalist Will Bunch (2020) writes: "America's addiction to militarism in the years since the Cold War has ultimately spent and—it now seems clear—wasted trillions of dollars to defend against hypothetical threats while leaving us practically helpless for the real ones." Bunch is criticizing both the unreality of the threats we have been fighting and our penchant to go to war, due to "addiction to militarism."

The war metaphor has gotten a good deal of use by several political figures in regard to the COVID-19 crisis. They highlight the intention to defeat the enemy. Taiwanese legislator Wang Ting-yu recommended a "wartime mentality" in regard to COVID for many nations, meaning a mentality that supported government aggressiveness and citizen vigilance around measures of mitigation (Hjelmgaard 2020). Andrew M. Cuomo, governor of New York State, referred to the United States in general (*Politico* 2020) and New York in particular (McKinley and Ferré-Sadurní 2021) as at war. He exhorted the National Guard to "kick coronavirus ass" (NBCConnecticut 2020), thus conjuring an embodied adversary that one could physically assault; actually, the National Guard was charged with aiding various capacity-for-care efforts, including building hospital facilities. The point is that the same metaphor, with the same set of meaning potentialities, may be used differently—emphasizing different aspects of the source domain—and for different purposes.

War metaphors are socially useful because they signal that the agent will give that effort their all. How does the war on COVID-19, as Trump uses the metaphor, construct the infection, those affected by it, and actions to be taken? What unsaid propositions does his usage cloak? In order to address such questions, the analyst first considers the source domain (war) and what things are like "there." Then, the analyst asks, what do these characteristics imply about the target domain?

Things are crystal clear: us versus them, valiant fighters versus enemies. Alive, embodied, and on the move, the enemy is to be stopped—and killed. In fact, to stop the virus—to actually win in the target domain—one must change the behavior of the hosts (or potential hosts). The viral "enemy" is inside living bodies and depends on those hosts for its reproduction. There is hardly any existential separation between "us" and "them" in this case, such as the war metaphor implies. Likewise, the virus does not take a single path, as Trump suggests ("the virus and its path"). Instead, the virus proliferates only as long as it dwells in bodies and these bodies interact with other bodies—providing new hosts. Trump's letter does not state any of this. Instead it says that "we are tracking the virus and isolating it." In literal wars, these moves make sense. In this "war" such putative moves are meaningless. The metaphor stamps out the facts of how viruses behave.[9]

Trump's desire is to "prevent further spread"—to stop the virus from moving—without stopping people from moving. His interests are jeopardized by the immobilization of people. Thus, Trump's letter to the governors is used not to summon effort but to declare to other decision-makers and the general public that the war effort is already successful, such that new guidelines would be issued about "maintaining, increasing or relaxing social distancing and other mitigation measures." It is time to stop fighting, or at least to stop fighting in the way that made epidemiological sense—by isolating potential carriers of the virus. Trump's rhetoric, including its erasures, serves the goal of declaring a victory—itself strategically understated—which current remedies would impede. The claim of victory in the war on COVID would elevate his standing *and* minimize the importance, for human life, of sustained measures against the virus.

Metaphors direct us to understandings from beyond the present object, while other figurative devices call attention to a specific dimension or part of the object itself. Metonymy is one such device.

METONYMY

Metonymy involves referring to someone or something by a term closely related to them or it. An example is "a suit" for a businessperson. Tim, discussed above, denied having "laid a hand" on the victim of his sexual assault. There, the hand stands in for the entire body. Through metonymy we "infer whole from parts or parts from wholes" (Gibbs 1999, 62). Like all figurative devices, metonyms invite meaning-making from the realm of dominant understandings, with the latter filling in the gaps that the metonym leaves.

Metonymic Storytelling

Stories cannot report everything. Omissions are essential. What I am calling metonymic storytelling indexes omission with conventional stand-in expressions or leaves out some events in a conventionalized sequence.

Just as we think and speak metaphorically, we also think and speak metonymically (Radden and Kövecses 1999). The latter insight in particular helps elaborate how narrative absences in the form of small stories or tropes generate a fuller-than-explicated sense of who is who and what goes on in the world. Experimental evidence shows that "people automatically infer appropriate, script-related actions when these are not explicitly stated" (Gibbs 1999, 69). Gibbs (1999, 68) offers as one example the statement, "John was hungry and went into a restaurant." Upon hearing it, the typical hearer infers mediating actions, such as physically getting to the restaurant. Gibbs comments: "When people hear this brief episode, they presumably activate their knowledge of the activities normally associated with eating in a restaurant and use this information to fill in the gaps to make the story coherent." Those who are culturally "in the know" do not need every part of an event series spelled out.

Parts and specifically events that are left out of stories may be the site of harmful action. Then, unsaid can provide cover and avoid any ideological tension surrounding such action. So it is that Steve, a man I interviewed in the spring of 1999, gave a condensed account of assaulting his wife. I had asked him if he had ever been involved in "stuff like assault kind of stuff or—in your lifetime?" to which he responded: "Yeah, domestic violence—me and the old lady—but, that's it." Later, in chapter 5, I reexamine this case for how *I* enabled Steve's erasure. Here I want to isolate very briefly what Steve offers as a tellable series of events.

LO: And uh—what was—what were the circumstances with that?[10]

STEVE: It's just—you know how you get into it?

LO: Get into an argument or—?

STEVE: Yeah, and all they got to do is pick the phone up and call.

Steve bids me to understand a generic series of (two) events that led to his arrest: a bilateral argument and his wife's "picking the phone up"—meaning phoning the police. This metonymic phrasing obscures his own actions. The qualification "all they got to do" erases the specific victim, conflating her with an amorphous group. It furthermore compresses all that brought the victim to summon help into a too-easy and malicious choice to harm him. Domestic violence has historically been removed from general view and consideration, in various ways and by various actors. That removal lives on in Steve's kind of storytelling.

Three main questions for analysis of metonymic storytelling in a zemiological context are:

- Would the excluded event expose an injustice or harm?
- How does the exclusion of characteristics of the protagonist construct them as harmless?
- How does the exclusion of characteristics of the Other construct them as harmworthy?

Chapter 4 offers another approach to exploring in terms of missing perspectives. That is, we can ask what the omission does or could accomplish, and we can ask whose perspective on "the story" is absent. It could be used in concert with the present study of metonymy.

The above three questions center on events and characteristics, as does my version of metonymic storytelling. I can well imagine other elements of stories being scrutinized, based on research foci: for example, which emotional expressions get storied and which do not. That line of inquiry could bear on how gender—which is tied to emotional expression, among other things—is culturally reproduced.

Code Words

Code words are especially concise metonyms.[11] Often one or two words, they are lexical referents for some broader, possibly problematic phenomenon or message. An example of a code word is "welfare," referring to a government subsistence payment of a particular kind in the United States. Its class-specificity is unstated—not given in the word per se but rather understood by convention. Entitlements delivered to social elites are excluded from "welfare" unless qualified ("corporate welfare") or signified as unusual or ironic. Kendi (2019, 154) observes: "Welfare for middle-and upper-income people remained out of the discourse on 'handouts'." Code words can be euphemistic, obscuring an uglier logic—a racist one, for example—with cover from expressions like "urban" and "inner city" (Lopez 2016; Sue and Robertson 2019). They permit negative evaluations (e.g., of the culture of the inner city) while dodging the appearance of racism.

The analyst asks what and who is associated with the code word, based on use in the present and the past as well as supposed historical and demographic patterns. The use of code words may also be traced back to a prominent speech or document from the past, a phenomenon I describe later in the book in terms of intertextuality (chapter 5).

Commonly obscuring potency, code words can also be used to represent some phenomenon in charged ways. When COVID-19 was first raging globally, president Donald Trump and right-wing pundits took to referring to the infection as the "Wuhan flu" or "Chinese virus," expressions that referenced, without spelling out, a xenophobic conspiracy theory of where the virus arose and how it evolved and spread. From a narrative perspective, the code words may be seen as tropes (Sandberg 2016), encapsulating and cuing a story, and potentially activating hearers the way that stories can.

Whereas "code" implies, in popular use, intentionality—presumably one *means* to speak in code, or encodes one's expression—the use of metonymy and figurative speech is not necessarily deliberate. Thus, for example, in the course of her fieldwork, Cohn (1987) adopted the codes used by nuclear defense planners. She describes her thinking as having become "militarized" (716), rather to her surprise and dismay. Instead of orienting to what users of metonymy mean to accomplish, an analysis of metonymy can be guided by what unsaid would accomplish. In this regard I endorse the concept of *interests*, which encompasses purposes—it points to desire—but whose investigation does not require evidence of intention.

The "welfare" example given above will help me illustrate. The US government has historically used different terms for different entitlements—"welfare" versus "government subsidies"—depending on the recipient: poor versus elite. The difference cues some ideological effort that may be surmised through information on material interests of the politicians who are active in reproducing that linguistic scheme. The unsaid context is that these politicians have been lobbied by those who receive the "subsidies." It is in the interests of the politicians to encode "subsidy" so that it goes nowhere near "welfare."

This methodological advice, to take interests into view when studying code words, applies to unsaid analysis of figurative expression more generally. Steve's interest in avoiding culpability and sanctions for spousal assault, and Trump's purposes in distracting us from his investment in a return to pre-pandemic economic activity, help analysts make sense of those speakers' metonymic ellipses.

CHAPTER SUMMARY

In general, figurative communication says one thing and means another. It implies what it does not state plainly. Literal meaning may be considered as supplanted by the figuration. Figuration gestures at broader taken-for-granted logics not enunciated within the text. Logics, as well as falsehoods, would be prone to critical appraisal if exposed outright.

The idea that figurative devices are deviant is something of a prejudice, and yet the prejudice serves unsaid analysis. The analyst treats divergence from some supposedly literal and full expression as efficiently integrating unsaid into the text. Thus, a story of raping refers to culturally accepted grounds for acting badly, specifically being licensed or compelled to do so. Those bases *could* go unmentioned because of the availability of metaphors for mutual obligation and physical immobilization. What is more, their being expressed metaphorically obscures the fact of their essential mutual incompatibility. That is, the contradiction is not so readily grasped.

As we have seen, figurative language can support harm-doing. Rape and other gendered harm is rooted in such unsaid logics concerning power and powerlessness. Trump's metaphoric rendering of the war on COVID-19, and related treatments of the battle plan and the adversary, have contributed to erroneous understandings of viral infection, promoting and obtaining consent for a turn away from mitigation measures that would save lives. The case of the war on COVID-19 underscored the importance of close scrutiny of target and source domain characteristics, given how common it is to construct a tough problem as a war enemy. Metonymic narration of a sequence of events—with the "harm parts" left out—can make harmful action sound more innocent than it is and/or render actors blameless.

The next chapter shifts focus to "outright" exclusions from texts. The challenge there is to establish that some persons, events, experiences, contexts, or perspectives are absent from the text but ought to be present.

4 Missing Subjects

> We were taught that Columbus *discovered* America;
> that "Indians" were scalphunters, killers of innocent
> women and children; that Black people were
> enslaved because of the biblical curse of Ham, that
> God "himself" had decreed they would be hewers of
> wood, tillers of the field, and bringers of water. No
> one talked of Africa as the cradle of civilization, of the
> Africans and Asians who came to America before
> Columbus. No one mentioned mass murders of
> Native Americans as genocide, or the rape of Native
> American and African women as terrorism. No one
> discussed slavery as a foundation for growth of capi-
> talism. No one described the forced breeding of
> White wives to increase the White population as
> sexist oppression.
>
> bell hooks, *Ain't I a Woman*

This chapter is concerned with "basic" but highly consequential absences. Someone or something, including ways of understanding the world, is absent from the text. The exclusion is not for the sake of obtaining buy-in or avoiding censure. It is not subterfuge, and it reflects no particular cunning. The point of the exclusion, if it has a point, is exclusion itself.

Persons and entire groups are marginal in, or altogether absent from, official histories of societies, social developments, and world affairs; and from academic publications, even those that are nominally critical (Barnet 2003; Ferber 2007; Namaste 2000; Stibbe 2015; Storrow 2013). They barely speak and are barely spoken of. Their actions are known only to them. The happenings of their lives and the circumstances in which they live are not publicized. Minority viewpoints—actual ones, as opposed to viewpoints that are presumed or fabricated—are excluded from law and policy development.

Such exclusion is itself injustice, but it also causes other injustice. As Stibbe (2015, 146) writes: "When erasure occurs across a text or discourse it forms a pattern very much like an appraisal pattern, except rather than appraising something as *bad*, it appraises it as *unimportant* and generally unworthy of consideration" (emphasis in the original). Unworthy of consideration equates to unworthy of just treatment and social support, even unworthy of commemoration after death (Butler 2004). In addition, harmful and unjust discursive exclusions make space for harmful and unjust discursive presences or propositions, as bell hooks makes clear in her monumental book *Ain't I a Woman* (see the epigraph to this chapter; 1981, 119–20; emphasis in the original).

This chapter distinguishes textual exclusions as persons, events, actions, experiences, contexts, and perspectives. Each of these subjects of exclusion is of central concern to critical scholarship, but analysis of such exclusion has rarely been subject to systematic discovery. To demonstrate how researchers might locate what I call missing subjects, I present rudimentary analyses of both sexual abuse and laws designed to help victims of sexual abuse. The analytical work I recommend has one asking the texts (1) whom they are representing and how, and which (2) events, actions, and experiences; (3) contexts; and (4) perspectives they feature.

Personhood, events, actions, experiences, contexts, and perspectives are mutually constitutive. Exclusion of any one of these six "subjects" tends to accompany exclusion of another. For example, a person who is unmentioned in a text is also unlikely to find her perspective represented there. The chapter considers methodology for each subject separately, notwithstanding the fact that they work in conjunction. Indeed, they form an ensemble in the context of stories. Persons, events, actions, experiences, and contexts are the stuff of stories, while perspectives supply stories' evaluative dimension. In view of the value of a narratological framework, the chapter draws to a close with a discussion of the social impact that people telling their own stories can have.

WHAT SHOULD NOT GO MISSING: KEY PROPOSITIONS AND A CONSIDERATION

As discussed at length in chapter 1, texts contain innumerable absences. Any meaningful message excludes, and moreover makes meaning *by* excluding. A zemiologically relevant unsaid analysis therefore must begin by establishing who and what should *not* go missing from the point of view of harm. It is surely problematic to assume consensus on such views. That is why I do not assume it. Instead, I recommend the analyst's setting out early in analysis, and again in their presentation of findings, just what they believe should be said and why, from some value-laden, theorized position on social goods and bads. Toward that end, I offer my own key propositions:

- The *persons* impacted in or by a text, actually or potentially, should have a place in the text proportionate to impact.
- The *events, actions,* and *experiences* that those impacted persons cite (or would likely cite) to make sense of the text and that which it conveys, should be featured in the text proportionate to impact.
- The *contexts* that those impacted persons cite (or would likely cite) to make sense of the text and that which it conveys, should be featured in the text proportionate to impact.
- The *perspectives* of those most impacted in or by a text, actually or potentially, should have a place in the text proportionate to impact.

Impact is central, as it is in zemiology. Yet, it could be said that the key propositions provide limited guidance concerning whose absence or silence should center analysis when more than one person is impacted by something or some text. Which impacted persons should receive the most attention? In some such cases the propositions may be taken as sensitizing rather than directive. But I offer for consideration a methodological privileging of subordinated subjects.

Imagine the progressive blog essay which, in taking some position on an argument, devotes little space to an elite perspective, whereas elites would be much affected by the argument. What standing does the elite critic of such underrepresentation have? In fact, elite perspectives are abundantly expressed at large and disseminated widely, whereas subaltern subjects—especially but not exclusively subaltern perspectives—suffer widespread exclusion. Such exclusion is at the heart of oppression and thus harm. Accordingly, the exclusion of elite perspectives is not a main concern of my version of unsaid analysis. Faced with multiple missing subjects, the critical unsaid analyst should focus on subaltern subjects.

I am not here arguing that subaltern perspectives are "right" and that they should be "the" perspective of any text. Rather, I am describing a method for turning up their absence in specific texts, from knowledge of their general, damaging, and unjust absence. Onto methods.

Persons

As a starting point, I propose that persons impacted in or by a text, actually or potentially, should have a place within it, and that those *most* impacted in or by a text, actually or potentially, should have the most central place within it. At a minimum, such persons ought not go missing from texts that concern them or that refer to events that concern them.[1] A follow-up proposition is that the text should represent persons impacted in or by it *the way* they would represent themselves.

Missing personhood can be distinguished as outright exclusion *or* as misrepresentation, the latter taking various forms. Outright exclusion is akin to "the void" that Stibbe (2015) describes. Persons are altogether excluded from discussions of general issues that concern them no less (and often more) than anyone else. In other words, they go missing from texts to and about the collective. A discussion of living with COVID-19 concerns homeless as well as institutionalized persons no less than others, yet these groups usually go unmentioned. (That they may be the subject of special reports highlights their broad exclusion.) Legal texts are a common and highly consequential site of missing subjects: consider "all men are created equal" in the US Declaration of Independence. Persons also go missing when texts universalize experience, treating one sort of experience as the general experience. Style and home magazines, for example, have tended to speak of middle-class lives as lives.

Misrepresentation is more complex. First, a text may marginalize persons, or include them minimally or secondarily. Second, a text may include persons but not faithfully or in their actual complexity.

An example of misrepresentation of the first kind comes from von Münchow's (2018) study of treatments of National Socialism and World War II in French and German history textbooks. She observes that both treat genocide of the Jews as a referent for Sinti and Roma genocide (36). Phrasing such as "Jews above all, but also Sinti and Roma," in the German textbooks contrasts with phrasing in the French textbooks, which "generally simply 'add' the genocide of the Sinti and Roma to the genocide of the Jews" (36). Both French and German texts set up Sinti and Roma victimization as a secondary dimension of the Holocaust.

Persons are semiotically constructed, or characterized, through a variety of linguistic means. To investigate what has gone unsaid about persons in some material, several critical discourse analytic procedures are useful. These include direct examination of quoting verbs, modifiers, and nominalizations (Machin and Mayr 2012).[2]

Through these procedures, one can ask what qualities of personhood are being left out of discussion.

Analysts may also deploy a narratological vocabulary with which to assess exclusionary representations. In the field of narratology, questions of representation include: Who is the story about? Who is the main character? And who are the story's minor characters?

Alex Woloch (2003), in theorizing character-space, notes that "discrete representation of any specific individual is intertwined with the narrative's continual apportioning of attention to different characters who jostle for limited space within the same fictive universe" (20). That is, attention/space is differentially distributed across characters. One can ask of nonliterary texts the kinds of questions Woloch asks of literary ones, including: "How often, at what point, and for what duration does a character appear in the text?"; and "How are her appearances positioned in relation to other characters and to the thematic and structural totality of the narrative?" (20).

In addition, persons might receive flat or shallow treatment. Their "thoughts, feelings, and needs" might be omitted (Alcántara-Plá and Ruiz-Sánchez 2018, 61). To assess such marginalization, Murray Smith's (1995) narratological framework is useful. Focusing on fictional film narratives rather than literary (written) ones, Smith contends that audiences are led to relate to characters through processes of "alignment" and "allegiance." Alignment involves access to what characters do, know, and feel (83) and seems close to what Woloch is getting at in the above discussion. Allegiance has viewers morally identifying with a character. In doing sociological unsaid analysis, real-world individuals substitute for fictional characters. The account given by Margaret Gullette (2017, xv) of the experience of ageism uses a narrative vocabulary and may be considered in narratological ways: "Slowly it dawns on them, the protagonists of their own lives, that they are becoming minor defective characters in someone else's story." Old people are not just "minor" characters; they are also "defective" ones. Younger people should neither align nor should they be allied with them, for as Smith (1995, 188) explains: "To become allied with a character, the spectator must evaluate the character as representing a morally desirable (or at least preferable) set of traits, in relation to other characters within the fiction."

Allegiance is thwarted when persons are wrongly characterized as morally culpable for what befalls them or as bystanders to their own moral concerns. Black children are regularly characterized as dangerous, their innocence discursively and thus legally denied; Sharpe (2016, 79) refers to "the impossibility of Black childhood." Certain rape victims are characterized as not virtuous and therefore not victims. Alternatively, agency is erased. Some anti-abortion bills and laws portray girls and women seeking abortion as victims needing government protection rather than as moral decision-makers. These legal texts construct abortion-seeking girls and women as lacking some information that would dissuade them from getting an abortion; in the case of minors, of being transported across state lines to get a legal abortion; and of being forced to have an abortion.[3] The question for inquiry into this sort of marginalization, in line with my follow-up proposition, is: Would these groups represent themselves as the discursive treatments do?

Events, Actions, and Experiences

Beyond the inclusion of persons themselves, there is the question of what they do and what they encounter. The question of events, actions, and experiences is the question of content—or *what* is being talked about rather than *who* is talking or being talked about. I propose that the events, actions, and experiences posited as central to a text should be those that cause the greatest impact on persons, and particularly subaltern persons, *from their perspective*. Alternatively, they are events, actions, and experiences whose textual representations could cause such impact.

Events, actions, and experiences are closely related. An event is generally taken to be what happened or is happening, usually delimited by place and time. An action is someone doing something. It may be conceived as an event, but with agency as the focal point. An experience is generally understood as how an event seems or feels to someone. Experience implies something beyond simply "what happened." So it is unsurprising that the term is also used to mean some sustained phenomenon (more than a single episode).

As discussed above regarding persons, storytelling admits to a great deal of variation as to who, what, and so forth. Something has happened, which is recounted in a story. What is the story about? Robert Aaron Long killed eight people in and around massage/spa businesses in the Atlanta, Georgia, area on March 16, 2021. Six of the victims were Asian women. Long's first stop, at which he killed five people, was the Youngs Asian Massage Parlor (Walsh 2021). At a press conference after the killings, captain Jay Baker of the Cherokee Sheriff's Office related that Long "was pretty much fed up, had been kind of at the end of his rope, and yesterday was a really bad day for him and this is what he did" (ABC11.com 2021). In that statement/story, "this is what he did" omits mention of *what* he did and to *whom*. It indexes and supplants the murder of eight people. This move, first, erases the victims, which, second, makes possible the view on the part of law enforcement that the violence was not tied to race-gender hostility.

"The elephant in the room" refers to an event, action, or circumstance that should be abundantly apparent but is not being talked about. Communicators may not be aware of some important event or circumstance. Not knowing about such things is a predictable result of not being affected by them. Or communicators have not bothered to notice them; they may do well by failing to become aware. Race and racism in the United States offer a ready example. Race is deemed not relevant in neighborhoods, workplaces, and classrooms that are predominantly white: observers "do not see" race. Alternatively, communicators may be intentionally trying to distract attention from one event or circumstance by highlighting another, a commonplace of political strategy.

Events can also be little or not talked about because they are common and understood as such. Alex Johnston (2021), a documentary

filmmaker, calls for "non-story-driven historical documentary practice" based on his archival study of the horrific and all-too-ordinary
violence, on September 6, 1913, against poor young Black men imprisoned at the Harlem Prison Farm in East Texas. Johnston tells the
story of their punishment for protesting work conditions at the prison.
Twelve men were confined to a small wooden box; by the time authorities released them the next day, eight had died of asphyxiation.

Whereas the Harlem Prison Farm incident is a vivid demonstration of the reach of state violence, Johnston points to its limited narrativity. Drawing on Hayden White's conception of narratives as
moralizing by nature, Johnston explains:

> As a "typical" event in the history of the Jim Crow South—the brutali-
> zation and murder of poor black men—the incident at Harlem Farm
> has evidentiary value to historians of the left, but no easily discernible
> narrative value. It offers no closure in the way of fomenting cultural or
> legislative change, and its tragic moral and ethical significance is not
> perceptibly different from myriad other incidents of the period.

Violence and more violence against the usual victims is not much of
a story—even, Johnston points, out in "histories of carcerality and race
in America." The "'unremarkable' nature of what happened to the men
at the Harlem Prison Farm doomed their deaths to obsolescence."[4]

If today activists would story these events, despite their painful
repetition and stasis, there is still the problem of the "scant archival
trace" (Johnston 2021). Events marginalized in the past inform
today's silences.

Alcántara-Plá and Ruiz-Sánchez (2018) point to conspicuously
absent events in the sphere of electoral politics. The authors observe
that Spanish political candidates tweeted about war and consequent
migration but not an urgent contemporary instance of these in Syria:
"Parties and candidates were able to send 57 tweets about migration
in 2015 without mentioning the refugee crisis. They could also pub-
lish 29 messages with the word 'war' without referring to the frame
everyone had in their minds: the tragic news coming from Syria"

(61). Keeping the statements abstract effects silence on "the real problems of the emigrants" (47).

The authors center the intention to be silent (27), or concealment, whereas my strategy, emphasizing impact, does not. The proposition that events and experiences discussed in texts should be calibrated to impact is a tricky one. Must we only dedicate attention to the *most* consequential instances of a phenomenon? This issue hits researchers right where they/we live. All inquiries, and reports thereof, limit their attention. The choice of how to do so is never neutral. Can scholars study "inner-city violence," for example, and set aside the violence that state actors do in the inner city? Can we talk about "child sexual abuse" and proceed to focus on abuse in homes and not in institutions? Can we discuss barriers to promotion at work for middle-class women and not barriers for poor women? I believe that the answers to these questions depend on what we identify as our focus and, moreover, give as rationales for that focus. I appreciate the researcher who candidly articulates the parameters of inquiry and explains these with harm and justice in mind.

These questions may remind some readers of left realist thinking within criminology. The left realists alleged that critical criminologists of the post–World War II period had sidelined interpersonal violence and other crimes, thereby forsaking victims, in order to launch broader critiques of criminalization processes and apparatuses. They insisted that "to say that present penal practice is unethical, antediluvian and counterproductive is not to negate the fact that crime is a problem" (Young 1987, 355). Unsaid analysis makes room for, and is concerned with, all manner of harms—broadly impactful structures as well as their local manifestations, large and small exclusions—and with both locally shared and canonical texts.

Not all harmful omissions are *obviously* harm-related. Even treatments of supposedly light topics such as so-called lifestyle or beauty, with seemingly trivial impact, can suggest that an exclusive kind of doing and being in the world is the standard, and thus erase from personhood those who have no such experience. For example, images of women at work generally represent office work as opposed to manual labor. More stories from more tellers, that portray other experiences, potentially undermine such hegemonies. A "Sunday Routine" series in the *New York Times* profiles "newsworthy" New Yorkers on the question of how they spend a typical Sunday. Most lifestyle features of this kind, and lifestyle magazines on the whole, imply the typicality of middle-class leisure and disposable income, used for example to pursue hobbies, buy luxury items, and eat at sit-down restaurants. Entire magazines dedicated to the affluent "interpellate" readers in this way, and little is thought of it (Althusser 1971). (Recall the *Marie Claire* article discussed in chapter 2 concerning regret for the text: "When the time comes, most of us will reach for anti-ageing beauty products.") By including stories from people who are not affluent, even those who are poor, "Sunday Routine" exposes and unsettles that ideological conflation of financial means with personhood. So it was with a profile, published in the midst of the COVID-19 pandemic, of a home health aide named Keisha Gourdet, who works so many hours on a typical Sunday that she is able to get less than three hours of sleep when the day is done (Strauss 2020). Many of us have been missing these experiences of "Sunday." When more generally representative "own stories" are disseminated, they can restore more persons to known personhood.[5]

Contexts

Context is sometimes used synonymously with *conditions*, but the concept is quite a bit broader, representing all that bears on how individuals live, communicate, and otherwise act. Context potentially includes conditions at macro, meso, and micro/individual levels, both past and present. These demonstrably shape how persons respond to things. My proposition for missing contexts analysis is: The contexts that impacted persons cite or would likely cite to make sense of the text and that which it conveys, should be featured in the text proportionate to the impact of both the text and what the text relates. As with the prior propositions, I consider this an analytical tool, however much it also states how things should be for the sake of justice and well-being.

The previous chapter considered an account of partner violence given by Steve, from which he excluded his own actions. Steve contextualized the incident in terms of a law enforcement reporting protocol that is heedless of his actual innocence, which his wife/victim took advantage of. The analyst can probe missing context via two key questions: What contexts are featured in the text? And are these the contexts that the impacted persons would cite?

Steve's victim might not build her story around his arrest at all. Steve's violence and its provocations might be the story's "complicating action," to use the language of the Labovian story model (Labov and Waletzky 1967). Like many victims of partner violence, she might situate that day's attack within a string of attacks. Generally speaking, perpetrators and victims tell different stories of "the" event that gets called crime.

Beyond so-called crime, it is often charged that some action or event has been taken out of context when it is being talked about, meaning that salient circumstances go unmentioned. Communicators supply different "contexts" depending on the situation of communication. Reporting of context is constrained by institutions. Legal systems are a definitive example (Atkinson and Drew 1979), limiting expression concerning the context of alleged infractions. It is commonplace for prosecutors to omit contexts that would highlight the paucity of options defendants faced at the time of the crime. Conduct is censured: the fact that it was the only or most feasible action path one could take at the time, is obscured. Similarly, concerning war, Machin and Mayr (2012, 42) describe "a suppression of information at the level of motives, of broader values and sequences of activity. There is also a suppression of the brutality of war, of the mutilating effects of the weapons used by these soldiers on the bodies of their enemies." To grasp these missing contexts, the analyst attends to what the affected parties deem important, accessed either by consulting them directly or through their accounts.

Analysts may also ask what historical events bear on the storied event or circumstance but go missing in the telling. For example, many criminologists have been quiet on the matter of mass imprisonment or the disproportionate capture of racial minorities by carceral agencies. They are silent on that essential context of their studies. It cannot be argued that patterns of "criminal justice" do not pertain to their studies of offending when they turn to official—that is, police-derived—rates of crime to verify the predicted "offending" patterns (see the case of Gottfredson and Hirschi, described in chapter 2).

Admittedly, my proposition concerning missing contexts is too coarsely fashioned, for it begs the question of *which* impactful experiences and contexts should be included in a text. For a working answer to this question, I turn next to perspectives.

Perspectives

A perspective, sometimes called a point of view, is an evaluative take on something. Perspective includes an assessment of which of the foregoing subjects—which experiences, which contexts—matter. My proposition for missing perspectives analysis is: The perspectives of those impacted in or by a text, actually or potentially, should have a place within it, and the perspectives of those most impacted in or by a text, actually or potentially, should have the most central place within it.

As before, the proposition, while ethical, is here meant to direct analysis by illuminating textual absences that do harm. Whatever is under discussion matters to some individuals or groups: their point of view should be reflected in the discussion and quite possibly should prevail.

Omission of certain perspectives is a paramount mechanism of ruling. Dominant groups maintain and legitimize their dominance in large part by "*excluding* rival forms of thought, perhaps by some unspoken but systematic logic" (Eagleton 1991, 6; emphasis in the original). In other words, these exclusions help achieve and maintain hegemony. For example, whereas the contemporary attack on "critical race theory" is blatant, prior dominant perspectives on race did the job of occluding the sociological insights of that theory by pointing to particular *racists* rather than systems that effect a racist order.

The question of (missing) perspective can be pursued in terms of whose perspective is spoken in a text—by virtue of authorship or by virtue of being quoted. Or, it can be pursued in terms of the more challenging question of the viewpoint or frame (Goffman 1974) of the text as a whole.

SPEAKERS

Perspective is roughly proxied by speaking. Those who author a text or are quoted within it usually give their perspectives. One's perspective may be voiced by oneself or others, or else it goes missing. Thus, the analysis of missing perspectives pays attention to missing speakers.

Teo (2000) finds missing speakers and thus missing perspectives based on discourse analysis of news reports on Vietnamese gangs in Australia. Neither Vietnamese people nor the gang members get to speak:

> Analysis of the quotation patterns and information sources points to an overwhelming disproportion of white majority voice against ethnic majority voice. This silence and silencing of the minority group are symptomatic of their powerlessness and disempowerment by the "expert," "authoritative" white community. . . . While the powerless are silenced, they are over-lexicalized with a wide but largely unsavoury characterization. As they are not given a voice to speak for themselves, they are literally at the mercy of those who do to say [*sic*] whatever they will of them. (23)

My propositions and questions systematize the procedure: take a position on whose perspective should predominate within a text and assess the representation of that perspective relative to other perspectives.

A caution is in order. Perspective cannot necessarily be read off of speech or the written word.[6] Consider the forced recitation of kidnappers' viewpoints (and demands) by hostages in videotapes sent to the media and governing authorities. Consider, too, prisoners compelled to confess or to frame other people. Gayatri Spivak's famous essay "Can the Subaltern Speak?" (1988) casts doubt on the possibility of the subaltern being heard, including the possibility of spokespersons for subaltern actors faithfully representing their views: the lenses through which spokespersons see the world get in the way.

Then there are the nonspeakers among us who have important perspectives that we are challenged to access. Nonhuman animals and the planet are regularly excluded from all manner of texts that affect them tremendously. One might defend such exclusions on the grounds that we are hard-pressed to communicate with and thus to truly know the perspective of nonhumans—as well as, for that matter, humans we deem inferior. Nonetheless, we human observers can be certain of the interests that nonhumans (like humans) have in *living and thriving*. Such interests, however broad, may be understood as indexing perspective, alongside any other strategies, now available or yet to be invented, for discerning it. It bears noting that people have, in any case, been remarkably obtuse about the perspectives of even competent human communicators.

Even when one seeks to translate in good faith, it may be difficult to tell what one individual speaking on behalf of a group really thinks. Groups and texts often have multiple perspectives, following the different voices they assimilate.

THE POINT OF VIEW OF THE TEXT

To say that a certain perspective is missing from a text requires at least some handle on what perspective the text *is* taking. Determining this perspective can be easier said than done.

Communications scholar Robert Entman's (1993) conceptualization of the framing of a text is helpful here. To frame, according to Entman, "is to select some aspects of a perceived reality and make them more salient in a communicating text, in such a way as to promote a particular problem definition, causal interpretation, moral evaluation, and/or treatment recommendation" (52). In other words, to frame a text is to put forward a perspective, or several. To locate frames within texts, one looks for "the presence or absence of certain keywords, stock phrases, stereotyped images, sources of information, and sentences that provide thematically reinforcing clusters of facts or judgments" (52). These are relatively accessible clues to perspective. However, perspective may be presupposed, that is, established as a given. It may be represented figuratively, as we saw in chapter 3. Or multiple perspectives may be presented.

Communication as a matter of course presupposes shared knowledge, beginning with the meaning of the words that one is using. Things get more obviously ideological where shared beliefs are concerned. As Polyzou (2015, 124) writes, presupposition does ideological work "by presenting certain beliefs as true, given and unquestionable, even if they were not known or shared by the audience before." Presupposition disguises partiality, treating one perspective as common sense or beyond dispute.

Presupposition pervades communication. The search for perspective benefits from a broad view of presupposition as manifest in "known or given information" (van Dijk 2014, 289), which van Dijk calls epistemic presupposition. The analyst can also discover presuppositions through linguistic particulars; van Dijk (2014, 285) notes that "linguistic presuppositions often have 'observable' manifestations in text and talk, for instance in definite expressions, clause position, topic-focus distribution, factive verbs, special adverbs and other presupposition 'triggers.'" Lexical choices can signal perspective. Every part of speech can do this work. Verbs having to do with speech may lend backing for, or conversely cast doubt on, what is spoken. For example, "the senator said" communicates less of a perspective than "the senator revealed" or, going further, "the senator admitted." The latter two phrasings suggest that the utterance is true, which can therefore be viewed as the perspective of the text.

The adversative conjunction "but" does formidable work in signaling that a more important, more credible, or redemptive perspective appears in the clause or sentence that follows it.

For example, Durrani (2018, 79) considers *Time* magazine's eulogy of a Pakistani president who came into power through a military coup. The eulogy included the remark: "His enemies described Mohammed Zia-ul-Haq as tough, uncompromising, even brutal. But those who got to know the late President privately discovered a devout, often charming man with a strong sense of mission." The ultimate perspective of the text is given in the second sentence, cued by "but" as well as the characterological contrast between more and less credible knowers. The leader's "enemies" do not have the reliable expertise that "those who got to know him" have, nor would they seem to have an interest in gaining better insight into his character.

To give another example, a comment such as "she is very dark, but she is a hard worker" (Sheriff 2000, 116) suggests that an undesirable quality communicated in the first clause is offset by a desirable quality communicated in the second. The unsaid here is that being "very dark" is usually at odds with being "a hard worker." A comparable, disparaging tactic is simply to place emphasis on an individual's having a desirable quality that is culturally constructed as unusual for their group—simply pointing out that the group member is "hard-working," for example. Knowledge of how the group is and has been constructed cues the hostility of the supposed praise. These gestures at unsaid may be considered intricate characterization, which I discussed as a kind of overstatement in chapter 2.

When passive constructions obscure exactly who owns a perspective, it can potentially be teased out by rewriting the text with active constructions. This move is familiar to educators and editors. Substitute "we argue" for "it is argued" and "I am raising questions" for "questions have been raised" or "it is questionable that . . . ." The perspective-holder, as subject of the sentence, is thus forced out into the open. In a dialogic setting, one can actually ask the communicator directly whether these substitutions hold (Petintseva 2019). The perspective, newly (re)attached to agents, is made more accountable since those agents' interests can be explored.

Perspectives are also very often conveyed in the context of *explanations*. The analyst focuses on the explanation or explanations the text offers for the actions, events, and conditions that it is purportedly about, such as violence by police officers. If explanations are not made explicit, they may be discerned from the solutions or next steps that are offered.

In recent years, political and other leaders in the United States have been charged with "bothsiderism"—that is, treating two contrasting perspectives on an issue as equally valid, helpful, or harmful. The charge implies that in granting equal legitimacy to the two perspectives, the text in fact aligns itself with one, ordinarily the one that reflects elite interests.

Turning to the matter of locating missing perspectives, and informed by critical social theory, unsaid analysts might focus on whether and how the perspectives of the subaltern (on the basis of gender, class, race, ethnicity, ability, sexuality, nationality, citizenship status, age, occupation, species, and so forth) are reported in or inform a text. How central are subaltern perspectives relative to others? "Most central place" aligns with the greatest proportion of textual space, hence a role for quantitative content analysis as a first step. Woloch's (2003) narratological question is relevant: "How much access are we given to a certain character's thoughts, and how does the partial enactment of this perspective or point of view fit into the narrative as a whole?"

CASE STUDY: WHAT GOES MISSING
FROM A STORY OF RAPE

The perspectives of victims go unheard as a constituent element of violence.[7] A story of raping told by Tim (pseudonym), which was briefly introduced in the last chapter (on metaphors and unsaid), highlights missing perspectives and demonstrates their analysis.

During the research interview with me, Tim described what began as consensual sexual activity: "She never struggled up to that point. You know, an' even—even when I had sex with her, she was respondin' to me."

By claiming that his victim did not struggle and furthermore was sexually aroused, Tim indicated that she was a willing, interested participant in sex. At that point Tim reads her perspective from the conduct of her body and not anything she says. The victim did not tell Tim in any way that she felt aroused. (Tim's reading may have been genuine or self-interested.) The only speech Tim attributed to the victim is as follows, which she reportedly expressed just prior to penetration: "I changed my mind. I don't want to do this. My boyfriend might found [*sic*] out."

Tim recalled far more about what the victim did *not* do and say:

> Like I said, if she would have resisted, if she just—if she woulda got up and got bold with me, I woulda ran out of that place, man. I never done anything like that in my life man. My—she would've scared me to death, if she woulda done that to me. But she was just quiet and passive.

These narrative counterfactuals help Tim establish his innocence (Presser 2008). The victim did *not* "get bold" and therefore suffered what she suffered, and Tim was not responsible. Tim called out the victim's unsaid words as the grounds for at least some blamelessness on his part. "But I—I was wrong, I did it, an' it was wrong but—even then—even at that point—she—she was a willing partner."

After Tim achieved orgasm, his acquaintance awoke from drunken sleep, crossed the room, and proceeded to rape the girl. Tim describes, "When I got off of her, he was right there," and reflects on his subsequent understanding: "You know, later on I was—after everything happened and everything, I felt bad for not gettin' that bastard off of her, but—because I figured she was just probably scared to death."

For the first time Tim entertains the victim's perspective, though it is connected to the other man's rape and not his own. It appears in a kind of coda to his own story.

Tim's story of raping shows us that perspectives get marginalized no less forcefully for being marginalized *discursively*—through misrecognition, discursive counterfactuals, and locating them outside of the main story.

The year was 1977. A variety of factors were, arguably more commonly than now, taken to invalidate the charge of sexual violence. Tim said: "So the prosecutor was havin' a hard time on a rape case, they have to prove force." The victim was questioned on the stand. "An' she didn't know what intercourse was; the courtroom started laughin', you know. I felt bad for her. But I was scared of this prosecutor." What is unsaid is that the victim should know the word "intercourse" and is worth mocking, disrespecting, and discrediting because she lacked that linguistic competence. Overall, what the victim did not say and what she could not say reduced her as a person.

Tim's story of raping casts his victim—she is not strictly speaking missing from it—in a way that denies her own perspective on her desire. In many discursive realms, rape victims disappear altogether. Historically, policy and legal edicts governing sexual and other physical abuse have addressed the violation in terms of elite men's property interests, thus placing victims outside of the story. Wartime regulation of rape is similar. Concerning the rape of Jewish women during the Holocaust, Sinnreich (2008, 2) writes: "Even when soldiers were disciplined for raping non-German women, it was for the breakdown in military discipline rather than the violation of the woman." Absences are co-requisites to reducing rape victims as well as perpetrators and downgrading the experience of harm via rape.

The concept of the rape myth is pertinent here but due for revision in terms of unsaid. Burt (1980, 217) defines rape myths as "prejudicial, stereotyped, or false beliefs about rape, rape victims, and rapists." Myths, according to Barthes (1957), are imposing. They are inherently conservative, as literary scholar Kermode (2000, 39) notes: myths are "the agents of stability." Rape myths are discourses—impactful through communication, embedded in social practices, and consequential even if their espouser does not actually believe them. Furthermore, and central to the focus of this book, they may take the form of negative space within communication. For few spokespersons of rape culture endorse rape in an absolute sense. Rather, they tend to proffer conditional acceptance of rape. The sexual assault is "not rape" or "not bad" under certain conditions involving certain victims, who are "not victims," and certain perpetrators, who are "not perpetrators." Clearly, a great deal of "not" is said. But also, a great deal is *not said*, such as about licenses to harm and what gendered bodies "must" do, as shown by Tim's story of his arousal and the inevitability of resolution through ejaculation. Accordingly, I would reframe as *rape mythology* that wide array of rape myths observers have identified. Mythology implies a collection or gestalt of myths. By rape mythology I mean to imply a breadth that extends to absences—a gestalt of texts.

Per my propositions, the victim's perspective on her own desires across the encounter with Tim, which directs his storied legitimization of the assault, should be central. But it is not. Tim's perspective dominates.

It might seem banal to point out that victims and victims' perspectives make spotty appearances in the accounts of those who harmed them. It practically goes without saying. Yet, victims' perspectives are also suppressed in advocacy, as we will see next in relation to child sexual abuse.

*CASE STUDY: MISSING VICTIMS' PERSPECTIVES
IN LEGISLATION CONCERNING CHILD SEXUAL
ABUSE IMAGERY ONLINE*

In the contemporary United States, at both federal and state levels, politicians have articulated rights that persons formally designated as crime victims have, including the right to protection from offenders and the right to compensation from the offender for injury or loss (US Sentencing Commission 2020; Tennessee Department of Correction 2021). We can evaluate these rights statements textually and ask whose perspective they take. The case of child sexual abuse imagery online (CSAIO) allows us to critically assess texts that would appear to be helpful to victims but stand to do harm by negating their actual victimization experiences (Little 2016).

In the United States, the federal Crime Victims' Rights Act of 1990 ensures, among other rights, the "right to reasonable, accurate, and timely notice of any public court proceeding, or any parole proceeding, involving the crime or of any release or escape of the accused." The treatment of crime as an event—cued by the definite article, *the*—is not surprising: one of the central logics of "criminal justice" is to distinguish victimization in terms of so many criminal incidents. Such logic is systemically unsaid. It is the common sense of the field of criminal justice to view victimization in this way and not in other ways.

Yet, CSAIO, like other crimes as well as legal harms, is generally not one incident—probably not in the first instance in which the images were produced, and certainly not in the way victims experience the harm, then and after. Looking at the experience in terms of incidents gets the experience fundamentally wrong (Martin 2015). Little (2016, 8) observes: "The harms of CSAIO are not mere events; CSAIO creates a *state* of harm for survivors. States of harm refer to conditions whereby the harm imposed is ongoing and incorporated into the life of the survivor." Victims say that living with visual records of one's sexual abuse, not knowing who will see and share these records, and those spaces being commodified—reduced to an image—are all part of the lifelong devastation of CSAIO. As one CSAIO victim said of photos of her assault online: "Anyone can see them. People ask for them and are still downloading them. Day after day" (Canadian Resource Centre for Victims of Crime 2007, 8).

Penalty schemes likewise fail to heed, and hear, what victims are saying. Justice officials generally measure the magnitude of the crime of trafficking in child pornography in terms of the number of images one possesses, replicating the degradation. Consider, for example, the Tennessee Protection of Children against Sexual Exploitation Act of 1990: "A violation of this section is a Class C felony; however, if the number of individual images, materials, or combination of images and materials that are promoted, sold, distributed, transported, purchased, exchanged or possessed, with intent to promote, sell, distribute, transport, purchase or exchange, is more than twenty-five (25), then the offense shall be a Class B felony."

It is not the victim's perspective, however, that the greater the number of images and materials, the worse the harm. Rather, the devastation seems to stem from ongoingness and uncertainty, as well as the knowledge of a network of victimizers—those countless viewers who are indifferent to one's suffering. The victim quoted above reflects: "Usually when someone is raped and abused, the criminal goes to prison and the abuse ends. But since (he) put these pictures on the Internet, my abuse is still going on." She asks: "How can so many people delight in the horrible things that happened to me?" (Canadian Resource Centre for Victims of Crime 2007, 8).

The number of images and materials has little if anything to do with the victim's experience—either in terms of initial assault or in terms of later insecurity as to who witnesses one's degradation. The victim is disturbed by the breadth and relentlessness of the invasion, not by vast holdings. In addition to gauging the offense in terms of number of images in possession, the statute emphasizes intent to traffic in them. Intent, a "guilty mind," is centered in Western criminal law more generally. Yet, the victim does not suffer more or less in step with what the viewer intends. Rather, the victim suffers a loss of control and an awareness of boundless, lifelong degradation. One victim reflects: "I know that these pictures will never end and that my 'virtual abuse' will go on forever" (7). On this conception, even the inspection of the materials for the sake of law enforcement constitutes harm. Clearly, victims' perspectives do not inform this nominal redress.

DOES TELLING "ONE'S OWN STORY" RECOVER MISSING SUBJECTS?

When subjects go missing from important texts, they are vulnerable to mistreatment or neglect. Shut off from the actual perspective of his rape victim, Tim operated on the idea that she wanted continued sexual contact. Without admitting the perspective of victims, penalties for those found in possession of child sexual abuse materials are meted out in a way that narrows the scope of complicity. Exclusionary and incomplete representation engender bad behavior and bad policy.

Would it help matters for the missing persons to tell their own stories? Would less harm be done if rape victims recounted their own exploitation, if marginalized persons generally related their perspectives on what has been done to them and what they have done? My answer is an assured yes. They, and the rest of us, need those stories. Crucially, however, there is no single story which is their "own."

We draw from culturally available genres, words, formulations, and forms—characters to be and trajectories to follow—to story our experiences. Even as we resist the storylines made available to us, we draw on some enculturated cache of them—of personhood possibilities. So I want to return to the matter of intertextuality. A single text "always relates to preceding or simultaneously occurring discourse" (Titscher et al. 2012, 23). The rape victim is compelled to speak more or less exactly in terms that investigators and the general public use concerning rape, such as to tell of events in the order that they supposedly happened, and not in terms of the salience to the victim. Lest we leave the critique at these hegemonic discourses, the rape victim can seek out counter-discourses, but they too will govern what can even be thought of as comment-worthy.

As discussed in chapter 1, each time we tell "our story" it is tailored to particular others and settings, and thus shaped in the telling (Herman 2009; Holstein and Gubrium 2000; Presser 2005).

Polletta (2006, 87) notes that "stories, more than other discursive forms, depend for their very coherence on the connections they forge between storyteller and audience and between particular experiences and more general normative standards." The fact that stories (and other texts) are not complete prior to social engagement is another reason why it is not possible to tell an altogether original story. "One's story" is a cultural imaginary that signifies authenticity, completeness, and self-ownership but cannot deliver these in any once-and-for-all way.

And yet, the story that one calls one's own, in one's own words, surely leaves out fewer subjects that matter to one's well-being than does the story authored by another. As Christian (1985, xiii) asserts, "If black women do not say who they are, other people will say it badly for them." Assuming storytellers want to tell the story, as opposed to being ordered or pressured to do so, they have an interest in striving for their own most authentic version of experience. They recount *their* perspectives; the contexts are those that *they* deem important in the event, however much the possibilities of thinking and saying are socially determined. Whereas storytellers use stock cultural codes, empowered storytellers are at liberty to use them in maximally creative and fulfilling ways. No wonder that victims aspire to speak of traumatizing events and faithful advocates wish to bear witness to the speaking—that both come to invest in "the restorative power of truth-telling" (Herman 1997, 181).

Beyond the simple fact of telling one's own stories, there is power in telling one's own stories in a manner and forum of one's choosing. Form, and not just content, reflects agency. Consider musical or poetic expression, science fiction, or alternatives. There is power in rejecting modes of expression that were fashioned in and by the dominant culture. There is also power in assuming the prerogative not to tell stories at all (Crouse 2021). Storytelling has been tied to healing, insight, rehabilitation, solidarity, and empowerment.[8] People who have been subordinated may very productively tell their stories, but they do not *owe* anyone their stories.

CHAPTER SUMMARY

Space in texts is limited, as is the capacity of audiences to focus on one thing or another. Including too many persons, events, actions, experiences, contexts, and perspectives would undermine the delivery of any cogent point. As Woloch (2003, 19–20) notes of some characters in literature, it "might disrupt the narrative if we pay them the attention they deserve." Yet, choices concerning what and whom to pay attention to are not politically neutral. Harm-promoting social arrangements are maintained inasmuch as some persons, events, actions, experiences, contexts, and perspectives regularly go missing. This kind of exclusion—as opposed to the kinds explored in previous chapters—establishes or reinforces social positions in a rather elementary way. It is simply detrimental to safety, flourishing, and self-determination to be excluded from the discursive outlets and instruments of one's society.

Textual exclusion of persons themselves, in which category I include nonhumans, is arguably the basis for the exclusion of their experiences, lived contexts, and perspectives. And yet, texts may nominally include persons but erase whatever they have going on. Missing persons become outsiders to their own social world—a harm in itself. They are kept out of discussions of whatever harm is recognized, and the harms they suffer are misconstrued. Discursive inclusion of persons is crucial in many ways, but it does not ensure discursive inclusion of any other thing about them.

As a starting point for the analysis of missing subjects, I advanced four key propositions, that persons, events, actions, experiences, contexts, and perspectives should appear in texts in step with the impact they (might) sustain from either the text or that which the text recounts/concerns. To gauge whether textual presence is "proportionate to impact," the analyst needs to assess both presence (or coverage) and impact (of both the text and what it relates). Some sort of quantification is advised. In regard to quantifying coverage, note that *equal* amounts of attention to persons, events, actions, experiences, contexts, and perspectives may be unjust if not commensurate with impact.[9] Assessing impact is no less challenging. Recent history has made it clear: claims to being bullied by words and claims to being censored ("canceled") are often offered in bad faith. They cannot be accepted unthinkingly. Hence the critical scholar deploys the propositions with specific attention to the subaltern. Accordingly, an additional consideration for all four propositions is this: whereas many persons sustain the impact of texts and the phenomena texts describe, the impact on the subaltern should be privileged, in accord with Gordon's (1997, 64) statement on the purpose of exposing ghosts: "Out of a concern for justice would be the only reason one would bother."

The analyst's own blind spots will influence the assessment (Lincoln and Guba 1985). For example, the analyst might not consider some stakeholder group as impacted by a text and thus as important to hear from or about. I might, seemingly innocently, overlook the friends of rape victims in a discussion of rape. My conception of "those impacted" in or by texts is based on already known, evidenced, and codifiable impacts. Analysts may decide to broaden that conception, for example, from rape victims to all persons who are at risk of being raped. They may set an explicit social justice agenda for the analysis. Inviting subaltern expert informants to weigh in on texts can be a corrective. People's own stories can also prove very useful for gauging missing subjects. They expose the kinds of events and experiences, for example, that have been little exposed.

However much they are socially constructed, people's "own stories" tend to be faithful to the propositions above. That is, they tend to center that which impacts them. And yet, discourse and specifically unsaid is clearly socially constructed. We arrive at our story forms, our figures of speech, obscuring idioms, textual exclusions, and all the blind spots mentioned above, as members of a community. That community includes immediate conversational partners and speakers and hearers of a common language. The social construction of unsaid is the focus of the next chapter.

5 The Social Construction
of Absences

Previous chapters have shown how researchers might go about identifying the impactful things that people do not say. The discussion has at many points pulled unsaid out of context. That will not do, for unsaid analysis is *sociological* analysis. Absences evolve from prior absences, guided or mandated by particular social orders, and in particular social settings. This chapter asks: What does the social construction of absences look like, and how can researchers discover it?

The chapter has three related foci. First, it examines the assembly of unsaid through input or lack of input by interlocutors. How much or how little communicators elaborate on something in talk settings is relationally, situationally constructed. My examples center on face-to-face influence in real time, but one can also consider input into written work through editing. Second, the chapter examines how communicative settings and discursive genres shape what gets said and not said, which again is the case for oral as well as written text. Finally, it considers the phenomenon known as intertextuality, which is referencing of other texts. According to Allen (2011, 112), "intertextual theory argues that texts and signs refer not to the world or even primarily to concepts, but to other texts, other signs." The fact that texts relate to other texts is foundational to critical discourse analysis. Unsaid analysis offers a unique perspective on the matter, as I will show.

INTERLOCUTORS

Interlocutors respond to what their conversational partners have said, what they suspect they are saying, and what they suspect they might say.[1] In so doing, interlocutors shape both said and unsaid. Interlocutors ask questions, pressure their co-conversationalists for answers, and gesture nonverbally. Their silences give speakers opportunities for, or seem to invite, elaboration and evasion (Presser and Kurth 2009). They fill gaps or leave gaps intact (Norrick 2012). They appraise silence as untenable or, conversely, as warranted. Tannen (1985, 109) highlights the social construction of silence in distinguishing between silence and pause:

> When is a pause a silence? When it is longer than expected, or in an unexpected place, and therefore ceases to have its "business as usual" function and begins to indicate that something is missing. When does talk become oppressive—that is, perceived to be in violation of appropriate silence? When that talk is causing the pause or silence to be shorter than expected, or omitted where expected.

Tannen reminds us that silence defies objective identification. It is a social construction, and its situated significance is highly variable (see also Jaworski 1993). Furthermore, whatever gets called silence is "a joint production" no less than that which gets called speech is (Tannen 1985, 100). Hence the utility of conversation analysis, to which I will turn presently. Traditional conversation analysis is focused on what goes on within the text. We can deploy its techniques while also entertaining the relative social positions of interlocutors, which are vital to the social construction of unsaid.

Powerful Positions as Shapers of Unsaid

Laws and policies, from government and other institutions, construct absences. Repressive regimes censoring anti-regime speech are at the extreme end of such influence. Even in more democratic societies, laws and policies often govern what can be said. A contemporary example in the United States is Florida's Parental Rights in Education law—known informally as the "Don't Say Gay" bill—which "prohibits classroom discussion about sexual orientation or gender identity" in elementary school classrooms (Florida House of Representatives 2022).[2] Beyond laws and other formal authorization, but tethered to them, is influence at the level of particular social interactions and texts. Discourses that condemn "political correctness" and "wokeness," for example, have silencing effects (Schröter 2019).

Some people are conferred jurisdiction over the expression of others, granted by their more or less stable positions. Parents and teachers come to mind. Fivush and Pasupathi's (2019) study of interactions between mothers and their young children highlights parental supervision of said and unsaid. One mother in the study discouraged silence by prodding her four year-old daughter to express her sadness around the death of a teacher. Another mother, who had asked her four-year-old son his feelings on having been socially excluded by his sister, "silences [his] interpretation that his sister is mean by simply invalidating it through laughing at his comment and then, at least indirectly, contradicting his interpretation by saying she is not mean, at least not all the time" (130). The authors reflect that "silence can be constructed through not allowing voice or through only allowing certain events or interpretations to be voiced" (130). That the one doing the allowing is the so-called listener suggests that communicative authority is partially concealed.

Interviews place interviewers in an especially active role in shaping silence, though that role has not been a focal point of social research (Gubrium and Holstein 2009). Interviewers ask speakers to weigh in on something and to articulate what is as yet unsaid. Their research participants defer to, or ignore, demands for information depending on the presumed status of the researcher. However unobtrusive interviewers may try to be, participants are inclined to engage them, such as by fashioning what they say to the interviewers' presumed interests (De Fina 2009; Presser 2004).

Other, non-interview settings activate particular speakers, giving them more of "the floor" than they grant to other potential speakers, in step with practical purposes and power arrangements. Think of psychotherapy sessions and academic conferences. Everyday conversations likewise vary in terms of the speaking roles of the co-conversationalists, with more powerful interlocutors tending to govern what gets said even when they are positioned as listeners.

Beyond patent forms of control, the mere fact that one is communicating to *someone* shapes the communication, because "the talk by a party in a conversation is constructed or designed in ways which display an orientation and sensitivity to the particular other(s) who are the coparticipants" (Sacks, Schegloff and Jefferson 1978, 43). The phenomenon of fitting what one says to one's presumed audience, known as recipient design, is central to conversation analysis.

For discerning how absences are facilitated by present interlocutors, conversation analysis is useful. The conversation analyst illuminates how each communicator proceeds from the just-prior securing of understanding. In chapter 2 I discussed the silent stakes of parties to a physician visit, as seen through Toerien and Jackson's (2019) conversation analysis. Social researchers can use the tools of conversation analysis to address questions tuned to the foci of the preceding chapters with an emphasis on co-construction, adding up to the query: How are exclusions, figurativeness, ambiguity, patterns of elaboration, presuppositions, and the like assembled, turn by turn, by interactants?

Leaving Gaps

The social construction of absences is achieved via an interlocutor's lack of intervention in the event that a first speaker erases something or someone in their speech. Harmfulness pertains if the glossing-over replicates legitimizing characterizations of harms, irresponsible agents, and reduction of victims. Not-saying takes all the forms that the previous chapters considered.

An example comes from an interview I conducted with Steve, which was considered in previous chapters. At the time of the interview, Steve was living in a halfway house while on parole from a sentence for burglary. Steve was relatively forthcoming with various charges, including one for domestic violence in 1988. I asked Steve to tell me about the domestic assault charge. He answered my question but failed to elaborate in an informative way, as seen in the excerpt that follows. I did not ask again for a specific account, but I asked for other clarification. The first four lines should be familiar as material evaluated in the previous chapter, where I discussed Steve's metonymic storytelling.

At the start of the interview I prompted Steve with: "I simply would like to know your life story—as much as you feel like telling me." Once he started recounting crimes, I asked for specifics.

> LO: Any um any stuff like assault kind of stuff or—in your lifetime?
>
> STEVE: Yeah, domestic violence—me and the old lady—but, that's it.
>
> LO: Yeah. How long ago was that?
>
> STEVE: That was before—hmm—I caught my case in May—it was about '88.
>
> LO: Um, in '88. Hmm. So how old—help me out—how old were you then?
>
> STEVE: [Unclear] it was '56—I was about thirty-four.

LO: And uh—what was—what were the circumstances with that?

STEVE: It's just—you know how you get into it?

LO: Get into an argument or—?

STEVE: Yeah, and all they got to do is pick the phone up and call.

LO: 91—call the police?

STEVE: Call the police. [Somewhat sing-song tone.] [Pause, followed by unclear statement.] Judge gave me six months [unclear]. The judge gave me six months, gave me a four-hundred-dollar fine.

LO: Hmm.

STEVE: So not much—

LO: Are you still married?

Steve's responses to my question about the circumstances of the domestic violence incident center on misconduct on the part of the supposed victim (or victims) and an unfair criminal justice system ("all they got to do"). Steve linguistically erases himself and his own agency, marking his subjectivity with the indefinite *you* ("you know how you get into it?"). Immediately after, he provides details concerning his sentence via a plainly articulated narrative statement: "The judge gave me six months." "So not much" may be seen as an evaluation and one that dismisses the incident. By Steve's telling, the judge supported his claim that what he did was not serious and/or his culpability was limited.

These discursive practices yielding discursive absences did not meet with any resistance from me. I did not insist on a fully specified story, though I did request other clarification in the excerpted exchange above and over the entire course of our interview. I did not return to questioning Steve later about his assaultive conduct.

Recall that dispute is generally deviant in conversation: interlocutors usually cooperate with speakers (Heritage 1984) and help them minimize threats to "face" (Goffman 1955). As for the fact that I was interviewing Steve: nonintervention is normative in qualitative interviews, as it is in research generally, where the general goal is to collect and not shape the data. It is therefore quite easy to find examples of nonintervention in data thus obtained. Interviewers may make repeated attempts to elicit answers to questions, but to go so far as to challenge answers is typically considered bad social science (but see Petintseva 2019).

Filling Gaps Selectively

Interlocutors signal agreement without voicing it by failing to contest pernicious statements or parts thereof. In contesting some of what their co-conversationalists say, they let some harmful unsaid things stand, as can be seen in an exchange between John McCain, then Republican candidate for president of the United States, and a supporter. The setting was a campaign-sponsored "town hall meeting" in Lakeville, Minnesota, on October 10, 2008.[3]

> McCain passed his wireless microphone to one woman who said, "I can't trust Obama. I have read about him and he's not, he's not uh—he's an Arab. He's not—" before McCain retook the microphone and replied: "No, ma'am. He's a decent family man, [and] citizen that I just happen to have disagreements with on fundamental issues and that's what this campaign's all about. He's not [an Arab]." (Martin and Parnes 2008)

Many in the media commended McCain for cutting short an affront to his political opponent, Barack Obama. They regarded his rebuttal as a "call for civility" (Romano 2008). Other observers recognized that McCain had constructed a dangerous message via unsaid (Russo 2018).[4] He facilitated the woman's unsaid message that Arabs are dangerous, not by leaving that message alone, which would facilitate the message more moderately, but by supplying its logical counter, that Obama is not an Arab.

Theorizing "positioning," Davies and Harré (1990, 46) write: "Who one is is always an open question with a shifting answer depending upon the positions made available within one's own and others' discursive practices, and within those practices, the stories through which we make sense of our own and others' lives." In the story told *in nuce* by McCain's supporter, his political rival has a questionable character because he is an ethnic other—an Arab. McCain immediately revises the story to position the specific rival, Obama, but not the whole despised group, as morally decent.[5] He does not say "because he is not an Arab," but the implication exists, because he sandwiches his remark between the indistinct "no, ma'am," and the indistinct "he's not." The rejoinder "he's not" focuses attention on factual accuracy concerning one individual as opposed to groups. Attending to how turns at speech adjoin with one another to create meaning, the analyst asks:

- What claims are made?
- What do they leave unsaid?
- What counterclaims are made?
- What claims are not countered?

The fourth question targets tacit agreement with claims. In effect, it probes conspiracies of silence.

SETTINGS

The prior section oriented to the editing of texts, such as by co-conversationalists. We can also ask how settings for communication invite, or discourage, the filling of gaps.

People variously censor themselves depending on the situation they are speaking in. Even seemingly banal prompts and questions, such as "How are you?", call for different kinds of elaboration in a public versus a private space, even when the same person is asking. One's workplace permits, discourages, and prohibits some utterances; a bar permits and discourages (and maybe prohibits) others.

Social media platforms likewise construct settings that govern "speech." Some say these platforms have fostered an "anything goes" atmosphere, superficially suggesting that less would be unsaid, but investigations of what remains unsaid would be productive. In addition to physical (or virtual) location, contextual cues tell us what sort of responses are being solicited. Highly relevant in this regard is pragmatics, that branch of linguistics which concerns language and meaning making within contexts of use. Pragmatics illuminates how much goes unsaid in altogether effective communication. One might ask a friend, "Would you pick up my daughter?" The meaning taken will very likely depend on whether one's daughter is known to be ten months old or ten years old. That is, with the appropriate contextual information, a competent English speaker will know that the request concerns physically holding the child in the one case and retrieving her from a remote location in the other. In this example, what is not said is that which is taken to be readily understood from the extralinguistic facts of the child's age and the interlocutor's knowledge thereof. Prior statements, in effect, give meaning to present ones. The example was relatively benign. However, contextual information can also include various harmgenic understandings, as I will show.

INTERDISCURSIVITY AND INTERTEXTUALITY

Communication scholars and discourse analysts, and less often sociologists, use the term *interdiscursivity* to refer to the deployment of cultural structures that pattern a present communication. They distinguish interdiscursivity from *intertextuality*. Koskela (2013, 389–90) writes: "Intertextuality can be defined as a text-level phenomenon describing how a text refers to other, prior texts, whereas interdiscursivity is understood as a more abstract kind of borrowing of features of discourses or genres in text or talk." Both interdiscursivity and intertextuality are social mechanisms for constructing absences.

Interdiscursivity: Cultural Structures

Sociologists have proposed an array of cultural structures, including genres, stories, codes, frames, scripts, and schemas, that codify how events and circumstances ought to be understood. Very generally, these direct people to think and communicate in certain ways, with implications for what they do not think and therefore do not say.

For example, when a story seems to fall into a particular genre, certain ramifications of the story need not be spelled out. A genre is a basic, collectively understood category within which a particular story may be said to belong. Philip Smith (2005) identifies four narrative genres—the low mimetic genre, tragedy, romance, and apocalypse—in terms of which international conflicts evidently get spoken of in civil society. Once social actors assign (or accept) a particular genre, they are primed to achieve (or accept the achievement of) that genre's supposed ramifications or action paths—war, for example, if the story of some international conflict fits the apocalyptic genre. "Stand your ground," in other words. Those words need not be used: the story's conformity to the apocalyptic genre does the saying, roughly speaking.

Like settings for communication, cultural structures require or enable certain gaps. In fact, settings and cultural structures are intertwined. Settings implicate particular cultural structures. In most consumer environments, employees are not supposed to communicate anything unfavorable about the merchandise (or food or service). But this rule is less strict in many (though not all) higher-education environments, so that a sociology professor could well teach about the futility of education for fostering social change. Ethnographic research can illuminate the institutional contextualization of absence-production via the typical genres, codes, and frames that prevail in the context. An example is the work of Cohn (1987) concerning the codes of nuclear defense planners. Such research uncovers exclusions and addresses the question of how exclusions are accomplished.

The cultural structuring of unsaid is of considerable sociological importance insofar as "culture" in this context generally means "the dominant culture." Here again we confront the issue of power and absence. Master narratives, discussed in chapter 1, center the issue of power via cultural structure, and specifically via narrating some phenomenon.

A master narrative (or hegemonic narrative) is a dominant and subjugating, usually pervasive, account of how things came to be a certain way or how they tend to go. Master narratives are said to "pre-empt alternative stories" (Bell 2003, 6; see also Clifton and Van De Mieroop 2016)—that is, they keep alternative stories from being told. Master narratives also exclude by highlighting certain aspects of experience and not others. Consequently, master narratives inspire some remedies to a problem and fail to inspire others. For example, master narratives of school shootings generally fail to mention that most perpetrators are boys or men (Kimmel and Mahler 2003). Thus, interventions in the school shooting example that address gender socialization would not come to mind. Victims, too, are constrained by master narratives about their victimization. For example, Polletta (2009, 1491) notes the limitations of advocates' stories of battering: "The problem with accounts hinging on battered women's syndrome, I argue, is that the tragic form taken by those accounts make the woman's plight seem either unbelievable or somehow her fault." A better story, she contends, is that of rebirth:

> The story line has made it possible to grasp the condition of living death that is something like that of coercive control. It has made it possible to understand both why the woman stayed and why she fought back. When told in the first person, the author's strong narrative voice has conveyed an impression of agency and reasonableness, even as she has described experiences of dependence and dehumanization. (1506)

One is influenced to see and not see one's own situation in the terms of the prevailing narrative. Polletta notes that "new stories are heard in terms of old ones" (1506), though old forms can effectively be tweaked to say something new and authentic.

Social actors may themselves point to some prior discourse as influencing their thought and speech. In my study of Jim David Adkisson, who shot and killed several people at a Tennessee church in 2008, I explored the two stories he told—one a personal story, the other his story of political conflict in America (Presser 2012). Both stories emphasized incipient ruin, and both obscured the abuses perpetrated by the heroic protagonist. Adkisson's story of politics in America drew on the ideas of right-wing pundits in the United States, and he credited them for much of his thinking, telling me: "If you want to know what I think, just listen to Rush Limbaugh." I did not analyze Adkisson's appropriation of precise texts from Rush Limbaugh or anyone else. I did assess that Adkisson's personal story of affront by groups he claimed to loathe, including African-Americans, homosexuals, and people he called liberals, maps onto a public story of such. What Linde (2000) calls narrative induction refers to "the process by which people come to take on an existing set of stories as *their own* story" (608; emphasis in the original). One's cultural environment is sourced for the existing story with whatever absences it contains.

Intertextuality: Borrowing Said and Unsaid from Predecessors

Intertextuality, again, describes the phenomenon of communicators quoting, paraphrasing, or simply "name dropping" others. For instance: "Whether people have read any word by Freud or not, they tend, nowadays, to speak of themselves in Freudian ways" (Allen 2011, 135). Texts are "full of snatches of other texts, which may be explicitly demarcated or merged in, and which the text may assimilate, contradict, ironically echo, and so forth" (Fairclough 1992, 84).

I am interested in two specific ways that intertextuality relates to unsaid. Both adopt the convenient notion that unsaid lurks as an entity. First, in referring to what others have said without spelling it out, often without crediting those earlier speakers and texts, a communicator makes a point obliquely. The earlier remarks were meaningful within a bygone context, and the current speaker can now gesture to that meaning and context implicitly. Second, the borrowed speech contains absences, which the communicator, in effect, inherits. These absences may carry ideological weight, in the very same way that some metaphor might condone harm and injustice, if the current speaker is unaware. For example, "there are more than two ways to skin a cat" presupposes that it is all right to skin a cat. The analyst asks: What was the original, contextualized meaning, to which the current text gestures? And what absences (e.g., presuppositions) does the current text owe to its predecessor?

Tracking intertextuality can seem like straightforward work, but only at first glance, since the analyst must recognize the source text. It happened that Jim David Adkisson himself named his sources. Useful questions are: Where have I heard this before? What popular pundits are speaking similarly? Where does this text more customarily issue from?

It can also be helpful to ask whether some part of the text diverges stylistically from the rest. It might be more percussive, poetic, or refined. The rhyme in Trump's "when the looting starts, the shooting starts"—not typical of his speech—calls attention to another voice. That voice (first that of Miami police chief Walter E. Headley in the context of civil rights protests) spoke even more explicitly in support of racist state violence (Sprunt 2020). For unsaid analysis, once the source material is identified, one can ask: What unsaid within this text is *also* unsaid within remote texts?

With the popularity of social media platforms, texts are transacted more overtly than they have ever been. Today's communicators routinely cite, quote, and retweet others. Huge social media audiences are so many investigators to chart influence on what is said and what is not said.

Far-reaching absences are also handed down intergenerationally. The descendants of those who are silenced may in turn silence their children so that the latter might avoid encounters with discrimination. Blix et al. (2021) tell of Blix's grandmother having been shamed by a teacher for using her Sámi language in 1914 Norway; the grandmother thereafter avoided speaking it. Blix's father subsequently learned to cloak his own Sámi identity. For both descendants of victims and descendants of atrocity perpetrators, Savelsberg (2021, 22) found that "silent traces transmit tacit knowledge of the past within everyday family life." Fragmented knowledge becomes even more fragmented as it is passed on. The Armenian American writer Peter Balakian was mystified as a child by a scarcely mentioned "old country" that was no longer; "when he sought to inquire, adults would change the subject" (Savelsberg 2021, 20).

The history of a nation or group is fashioned based on texts that were partial from the start. They held back on things, given the strictures and prejudices of their time. Even oral histories track only what the storyteller knew and could know. On what other basis could history ever be written? The point is that exclusions start somewhere, and specifically that they start somewhere *else*. Textual gaps are beholden to broader discourses.

CHAPTER SUMMARY

This chapter deliberated on the social construction of unsaid. Whereas large-scale, formal structures such as political systems and laws are immensely influential, I focused attention on the contribution to unsaid of other people and discursive structures.

Interlocutors co-construct what gets said and what is left unsaid. When weighing in substantively on emergent meaning, they may correct some aspects of an emergent logic and not others, in that way honing a particular, taken-for-granted understanding. Social positions, such as parent or physician, confer the authority to guide and correct, often but not always subtly. In general, though, interlocutors tend to avoid confronting speakers on significant gaps in what they say. Goffman (1955) suggested that interlocutors tend to help one another make a positive or at least acceptable presentation of self. Hence Murray and Durrheim (2019b, 6) observe: "Avoidance is a dialogical accomplishment whose success depends on hearers playing their part, allowing the unstated topic to slide past without notice to be replaced with another, more acceptable one." Silence or minimal commentary from the other party may be construed by speakers as absence of judgement.

At the level of constructing one's statement, cultural structures such as genres and master narratives pattern what is permissible and even thinkable to say. Such patterning may be called interdiscursivity, which was contrasted with intertextuality, or the referencing of other texts. Interdiscursivity and intertextuality feature in all communication. The point for this book is that they allow present communicators to avoid spelling out all the ramifications and messages of the borrowed form or text. Among other things, shorthand characterizations of demonized others run on textual gaps, and these are handed down.

What people do not say is, in large part, in the eye and ear of the beholder. What lay and professional analysts take to be a gap in text or, contrariwise, what they take to be an absence of gaps (which is to say, coherence) is tied up with their own culture, their enculturation, and their positionality. The fact that meaning is socially constructed is the reason I would not use the term *decode* in regard to unsaid analysis. That would imply that the text, including its codes, is accessible in some once-and-for-all way. Instead, to borrow Murray and Durrheim's (2019b, 8) term, unsaid is "slippery." Unsaid analysis must be a humble exercise, as must research generally. Hence, again, I would note the importance of rigor as well as openness concerning how one worked through the text to arrive at inferences.

6 Concluding Remarks: Boundless Texts, Better Worlds

No all-inclusive text can be produced or even imagined. What is not being said in any instance or parcel of communication is boundless, but that has not prevented observers from pointing "it" out and giving "it" form. Hidden agendas, unspoken assumptions, and silenced viewpoints are regularly commented upon in critical discussion, both popular and academic. A new cadre of researchers aims to systematize the analysis.

I have set out strategies to analyze unsaid that follows from configurations of power and serves configurations of power. Unsaid underwrites oppression and suffering. That kind of not-saying can and should be a target of social justice activism. This final chapter recaps the methodological strategies set out in the book, engages critical questions about unsaid analysis, and considers how to intervene in silences.

METHODOLOGICAL STRATEGIES

Unsaid analysis is an interpretative and thus a culturally specific endeavor. The researcher brings particular social theories and world-views to bear. The analysis is partial, as all analyses are: the analyst should reveal *how* it is partial, as far as they can determine. If clearly executed, with assumptions communicated, the analysis can be replicated and judged for its soundness.[1]

My methodology orients to two kinds of absences: unsaid truths about power and harm; and missing subjects, the latter having to do with excluded persons, events, actions, experiences, contexts, and perspectives. Few works in unsaid analysis have brought these two discursive phenomena together into one methodological approach.[2] But I come from criminology and have criminological preoccupations, hence this merger. The conceptual foundation of the methodology is that not-saying does and conceals harm and injustice.

The study of unsaid truths about power and harm begins with the text and tracks back to unsaid using linguistic principles and knowledge of social and political contexts. For example, the study of overstatement and understatement begins with attention to patterns of elaboration, such as patterns that compromise clarity. Subsequently the question is asked: What ideological or self-exculpating work is the leaving-out doing? In contrast, the study of missing subjects begins with ideas about who and what should be present within a text. I proposed that persons, events, actions, experiences, contexts, and perspectives should be featured in a text insofar as the text and what it represents impact them. If the impact is widespread, subordinated persons should receive first consideration.

Research methods can and should be adapted to particular social phenomena and particular discursive activities. I anticipate that close case studies can help illuminate how it is that subaltern speakers have broken through the silence and exposed mystification. Specific, resistance-oriented questions can be asked of texts: for example, how are gaps used strategically to make counterclaims?

My approach to unsaid analysis has, in effect, advanced a view of texts as boundless. Researchers might usefully work from a notion of the text beyond the verbal. Intonation has traditionally been treated apart from text, though the demarcation is problematic, for intonation can very effectively convey meaning without "speaking." An example from Steve's metonymic storytelling about assault (see chapter 3) is his prosodic shift in recounting his partner's summoning help: "Call the police." My field notes indicate that he used a "sing-song voice," whose unsaid meaning, I believe, is that the summoning is a bit ridiculous. In addition, nonverbal behavior speaks; "talk is interwoven with gesture, facial expression, movement, posture to such an extent that it cannot be properly understood without reference to these 'extras'" (Fairclough 1989, 27). Intonation, cadence, and gesture characterize spoken communication, whereas in written communication such things as punctuation and paratext (e.g., titles or cover art) may be considered analogous. These tend to be viewed as extra or extraneous. What messaging do they do? Unsaid analysts can address that question.

CRITICAL ISSUES FOR UNSAID ANALYSIS

I hope to have inspired some thinking about the scope as well as the limits and limitations of unsaid analysis. In regard to the latter, I want to entertain five critical issues, which I present as possibilities that could put something of a damper on unsaid analysis: (1) absences have a bright side that the methodology neglects; (2) presences are also indeterminate, so unsaid analysis operates from a too-convenient fiction; (3) perhaps material structures matter more than both said and unsaid; (4) perhaps explicit statements matter more than tacit communication; and (5) *calling out* unsaid is itself used to do harm.

The Bright Side of Absences

For literary scholars aligned with reader-reception theory, as well as rhetoricians, textual gaps activate readers/audiences. Gaps extend an invitation to imaginative engagement in what the text means.[3] They arouse openness, creativity, and agency. For anarchists, collective action that is spontaneous and organic thrives on little being spelled out: "ambiguity and confusion elude containment" (Ferrell 2018, 67). Likewise, and as explored in chapter 1, silences may be a tool of resistance in the hands of subordinated persons.

In contrast to these views, this book patently accentuates the negative. It considers silences/gaps/absences as bad things. I am aware of the bad things in the world by training. Beyond me and this book, I would say that a sociological unsaid inquiry will indeed tend to lean toward the negative. Opotow and colleagues (2019, 120) put the matter well: "Silencing, as an active process of censorship, hollows out a discursive and psychic vacuum, but it also animates and sucks in stereotypes, anxieties, fears, and projections to fill the void." In other words, textual gaps are prone to being filled with that which prevails in the culture. That is not to say that gaps are necessarily "bad," but that they are risky.

What positivity this book has to offer, it achieves by mapping out a mode of resistance to unsaid. It offers set of strategies for exposing harmful gaps. It is rather little occupied with the kind of resistance that *exploits* gaps. Whereas silence can serve and has served large and small forms of resistance, a more cheerful researcher than I am will dwell there.

Presences Are Also Indeterminate

Unsaid analysis conjures presences as a foil. The idea is that what is said is "there"—in ink, on the recording, on video—and unsaid is not. The implication in turn is that what is visible and audible has a stable existence. But the words and images that are *there* are not, in fact, stable. Their uptake and impact depend upon language and its interpretation, both of which vary across historical time, setting, and interpreters. It is therefore hard to pin down the original or final version of a text. It is not necessarily anywhere. Discourse analysis is itself grounded in the notion that the said is not determinate; it "highlights the precarious nature of meaning" (Hardy, Harley, and Phillips 2004, 20).

For the most part, though, I have set aside the sweeping issue of the evanescence of meaning for the sake of practical inquiry. I have treated said and unsaid as though they sit still for a while.

If I have reified unsaid, I am in good company. Regular people, including activists, refer to silence as an entity. Alternative perspectival possibilities include Jenny Edbauer's (2005) theory of rhetorical ecologies, "co-ordinating processes, moving across the same social field and within shared structures of feeling" (20). It may be very helpful to shift to that sort of outlook, to dwell in the idea that some particular form of unsaid takes up only temporary residence in texts. It is animated through active, situated interpretation—through vivid presences.

Not surprisingly, theorists of great imagination have unsettled the divide between absence and presence. The present is said to be haunted by absences—things denied as well as potentialities (Freeman 2002): "the ghost is a living force" (Gordon 1997, 179). Conversely, many supposed presences are ignored and thus, in effect, become absences. Or too much presence undermines meaning, creating absence. As discussed in chapter 2, through "cacophonous commemoration," speech nominally meant for remembering is actually designed for forgetting (Vinitzky-Seroussi and Teeger 2010, 116; see also Vincent 2010). More can be less where overstatement is concerned. A future critic could reasonably question what exactly unsaid analysis chases down.

Material Structures

Voting laws that keep some groups of people from voting shape power relations and do harm, however those laws are talked into being. Likewise, a city's lack of sufficient affordable housing is a problem for low-income people regardless of how it is or was spoken about in the course of urban planning. Wars depend on alliances, resources, and capacities; as journalist Thomas L. Friedman said: "Wars are really defined and decided by things with weight, not by words in the air" (Garcia-Navarro et al. 2022). So it could be charged that unsaid analysis is too far removed from analysis of the real things that keep people down and cause them to suffer.

This critique is not new to cultural sociologists. And their response is fairly consolidated. Material structures operate—they come into existence and produce their effects—discursively, just as discourses operate, and have influence, materially. As Philip Smith (2005, 209) says of war: "The 'enemy' and 'interests' require cultural patterns for their very recognition." Thus, in the voting example, restrictions are generally sold to the public in some way, which entails, among other things, gaps in government statements about election fraud. Likewise, a zoning policy statement that neglects to mention impacts on homeless people is surely bound to the exclusion, intended or not, of homeless people from town hall meetings. (Do politicians make sure homeless people know about their public forums?) Subsequently, zoning out homeless people is tolerated, just as homelessness itself is, through discourses and discursive practices.

Friedman's contrast between "things with weight" and "words in the air" is evocative and popular but glosses over the fact that words have weight and are rooted in weighty things. To quote cultural sociologists Alexander and Smith (2002, 147), "cultural forces combine or clash with material conditions and rational interests to produce particular outcomes." I am convinced that *missing* texts are likewise cultural forces, that they likewise have weight and are rooted in weighty things. Analysts may choose not to direct attention to this level of social life. They may deem urgent situations as calling for attention to factors that are pronounced. Nonetheless, there can be no doubt that inconspicuous factors also shape the situation, and dramatically so. To discern them requires imagination, such as sociology brings to all its endeavors (Mills 1959).

Does Unsaid Even Matter Much?

One could argue that unsaid matters less than other things, that communication that conceals and excludes has only limited impact. One might situate the critique historically: perhaps unsaid does not matter very much in these times. Alternatively, perhaps unsaid does not matter much generally, because people are primarily held accountable for what they say, and not what for they *do not* say.

Allegedly, public discourse has become blatantly divisive (Baker and Rogers 2018; Hoggan 2019). Brazen name-calling, whether in the context of jousting between world leaders or chats among teenagers, is said to be abundant. A disturbing amount of political communication, from the heights of power, designates enemies in explicit terms (Smith 2019) and moreover unambiguously invites physical violence against the opposition (*Guardian* 2016). In the later years of the Trump presidency, the mainstream American news media seemed to have finally taken notice of the role of language in fomenting mass harm, with a focus on words or expressions that agents of harm appear to have lifted from influencers: "a shared vocabulary of intolerance" (Peters et al. 2019). It is often noticed that leaders are nowadays "saying the quiet part out loud"—that patently racist speech, in particular, is no longer forbidden. Why explore the role of omissions in engendering harm when today's harm owes so much to what is said explicitly?

A second, related point is that only explicit communication stands a chance of being sanctioned—the proverbial cry of "Fire!" in a crowded theatre. Perhaps, if implicit communication is difficult to discern—hence this book as guide—unsaid critique does not promise much justice or redress. Furthermore, if it is collectively sourced (as chapter 5 took pains to show), it is difficult to hold anyone accountable for it.

My response, first, is that absences play a central role in communication, *including* most if not all communication that is boldly aggressive. Calling someone "a loser" (President Trump's inclination) may seem entirely forthright. However, it does not announce one of its essential ideas, which is that life is a contest one wins or loses, and therefore that such a person as a "loser" exists. The essential idea and its supporting values construct the insult. Failing to explicate the essential idea and supporting values assures a level of acceptability. One muses, "Well, I guess he's a bit right that that guy is kind of a loser." Attention is directed away from the malignant but unsaid foundations.

I would offer two additional examples of unsaid bolstering what is said. Margaret Gullette (2017, xvii) ties ageist messaging to "glossy, loud propaganda" and "despicable falsehoods" in the mass media, and indicts an array of insults, assaults, and outright incitements for older people to die. Statements to the effect that old people are burdensome and marginal may be blatant, reflecting and reproducing what is arguably the last widely tolerated system of oppression or "ism." However, surreptitious signifiers, such as not being represented at all within discussions of "normal" living, seem acceptable, if they seem like anything at all. The general absences make way for the blatant putdowns: the latter have no counterweight.

Conspiratorial thinking, such as now seems to be inseparable from far-right ideology, offers a second example of the power of unsaid to hone what is said. Today's conspiracy theories send clues or coded alerts (so-called "breadcrumbs" in the case of the right-wing network known as QAnon) to promote recognition of allies and to mobilize action. McIntosh (2020) observes:

These white supremacists are closely parsing Trump's tweets for secret messages, thinking, for instance, that his announcement that he and Melania had COVID-19 and would get through it "together" indicated Hillary Clinton would be arrested at last—"to-get-her," get it? But such desperate hunts for clues attribute too much crypto-sophistication to Trump. What Trump is really saying has been tragically closer to the surface all along.

Whereas the white-supremacist group focuses on mythology concerning "what is"—various forms of alleged violence and corruption by the other side—the fiction of the cover-up does important work. The clues create community. They invite participation as followers try to spot the latest sign of something. The clues also lend the struggle an alluring tension.

In short, even in this age of blatantly expressed hostility, disinformation, misinformation, and conspiracy theories—holding back, neglecting to mention, excluding, and insinuating matter. Both said and unsaid communicate.

It is true that people are not generally judged for what they do not say (and more generally for what they do not do). But that fact only confirms that unsaid is exactly the kind of loophole through which communicators avoid accountability and get away with abuses. The loophole is informal and formal. For example, conservative commentator Bill O'Reilly (2019) defended Donald Trump against charges of racism, tweeting: "While researching my upcoming book 'The United States of Trump,' we could not find one example of the President discussing skin color in a pejorative way or promoting Caucasian dominance."

O'Reilly brings the evidence of what Trump said. In the legal sphere, an exclusive focus on what gets said counters allegations of incitement or hate speech. The second impeachment trial of Donald Trump brought to the fore considerations of whether figurative phrasing should be taken seriously. "Trump has almost always offered mixed messages that provide him plausible deniability while suggestively alluding to violence by his supporters or, at least, painting a drastic enough picture that might lead to such drastic measures" (Blake 2021). Figuration communicates no less than literal words, and furthermore constructs its own buffer against criticism.

Because social censure and legal penalties are sometimes attached to saying but only very rarely to not-saying, the fact of not-saying is exculpatory where hate speech and instigation are concerned. Some observers judged that Trump did not, in fact, incite the attack on the Capitol of January 6, 2021, because he did not *explicitly* bid it: "The president didn't mention violence on Wednesday, let alone provoke or incite it" (Shapiro 2021); "There was no call for lawless action by Trump" (Turley 2021).[4] The implication is that only positive speech is actionable. Unsaid analysis, not just by scholars but also by public analysts and citizens, is necessary to begin to penetrate that buffer.

Harmfully Calling Out Unsaid

Social actors are themselves attuned to what is unsaid. Calling out unsaid is one strategy for gaining political advantage. The calling-out can serve harmful or emancipatory ends. For example, conspiracy theories of various stripes assert that some wicked project is being hidden, truths about it suppressed. Hence witch hunts, pogroms, lynchings, and QAnon. Organized responses to the antiracist Black Lives Matter movement proclaim that Blue Lives Matter (the color blue representing police officers) and All Lives Matter. These slogans imply that Black Lives Matter implicitly denies the worth of other lives. The "calling out" positions the Black Lives Matter movement as hostile and aggressive and the counter-movement stakeholders as its victims.

Or, unsaid is "called out" to excuse one's own actions. Offenders excuse their harmful actions on the grounds that those they harmed did not protest. At the extreme, they allege that victims' non-speech invited the harmful actions. Rape is an exemplar: if rape victims did not say certain things during the event, the logic goes, they were not actually victimized. Hence Tim's self-defense on the basis of the victim's not-doing and not-saying, previously considered in chapter 3:

> Like I said, if she would have resisted, if she just—if she woulda got up and got bold with me, I woulda ran out of that place, man. I never done anything like that in my life man. My—she would've scared me to death, if she woulda done that to me. But she was just quiet and passive.

If pointing to what has not been said can be used to deny guilt, it can also create distance from problematic positions. Politicians have been known to remark on what they are not concealing. An example is Richard M. Nixon's refutation of speaking in racist code. Accepting the nomination for Republican candidate for president in August of 1968, he pronounced:

> The wave of crime is not going to be the wave of the future in the United States of America. We shall re-establish freedom from fear in America so that America can take the lead of re-establishing freedom from fear in the world. And to those who say that law-and-order is the code word for racism, there and here is a reply: Our goal is justice for every American. If we are to have respect for law in America, we must have laws that deserve respect.

Nixon references the possibility of covering something up—of not saying something ("the code word for racism")—in order to deny doing so. He preemptively denies unsaid as a means to deny the racism of his planned policies.

Speakers also reference the possibility of some hypothetical, less authentic speech to highlight their own authenticity as communicators. Conservative radio show host Rush Limbaugh (2018) made this illustrative remark on immigration: "Without sugarcoating it, the objective is to dilute and eventually eliminate or erase what is known as the distinct or unique American culture."

The introductory clause "without sugarcoating it" suggests that there is a more cautious statement that Limbaugh *could* make about

Democratic policy aims that would not be as genuine as the state-ment he *is* making. Both Nixon and Limbaugh direct attention to what they could say but are not saying. These counterfactuals are negative referents that construct the actual statements and their speakers as reliable.

In short, calling out unsaid is a strategy used for good-faith and bad-faith efforts, and for progressive and reactionary goals. Along these lines, Murray and Durrheim (2019b, 10) observe that "analyses and diagnoses of silences and absences are themselves silencing": "bringing one silence into view can have the effect of silencing other features of context and the perspectives that could make them visible." How can "our kind" of unsaid analysis be distinguished from regres-sive counterparts? Research with integrity, on unsaid and everything else, brings theory and data to bear. It is conducted as meticulously and as transparently as possible. Analysts expose and challenge their own presuppositions and initial readings. Analysts make clear that they are not in the business of discovering truths. Unsaid analysis foregrounds interpretivism. I do not believe the same can be said of the cynical theories and self-positioning described above. There, methods are reckless, evidence is eschewed, and anecdote is every-thing. Alternative views are derided rather than considered. If unsaid is to be called out, it must be with humility and care.

INTERVENING IN SILENCES

My methods are designed to help analysts track unsaid in texts. Going forward, the methods could contribute to intervening in silences wherever they surface in the world. Intervention takes the form of critique *or* challenging speakers themselves to contemplate their silences and the effects of those silences.

Social researchers have traditionally tried to intervene as little as possible in whatever social scene they are entering to study.[5] At the same time, researchers typically seek greater understanding when things are unclear, with requests for clarification or follow-up questions and prompts. As such, they do broach silences, but selectively.

The criminologist Olga Petintseva (2019) offers a model of intervening during research interviews for the sake of targeting interviewees' biases. She calls the model Socrates Light, "in which the researcher enters a discussion and attempts to uncover and challenge tropes and silent interpretative schemata" (105). An example from her study is an interviewer responding to a non-Roma social worker's characterization of Roma parents as not taking a child's criminal involvement seriously: "How can you assess . . . that the parents do not see the seriousness of the offences? Do they say this explicitly?" The intervention has the interlocutor disallowing the inconspicuous taken-for-grantedness of biased cultural notions. Again, norms of proper interviewing, as well as everyday politeness—our inclination to help those we interact with "save face"—inhibit such an intervention. But intervention also depends on whether interlocutors recognize something as unsaid in the first place. It is difficult to grasp silences in the communicative moment. Zerubavel (2019, 61) explains: "Hearing silence is much easier in retrospect, after it has already been broken." How then to intervene?

As Zerubavel suggests, it is easier to "hear" silence in a text when one has some time to reflect on it. Written, as opposed to oral, texts generally allow for such time. When one is hearing spoken words, only seconds are available to launch a challenge before the conversation has moved on. In this circumstance, certain habits are useful. People can develop a habit of paying close attention to the predicates of others' remarks—what they presuppose. They can develop standard, ready-to-go rejoinders, such as "I'm thinking about what that assumes" or "I'm not sure everyone would agree with your premise."

Heightened awareness of exclusions and the ways they become manifest locally can help. Some people may always be better at noticing exclusions by virtue of the fact that they are so often excluded. They are well positioned to intervene in the relevant text in the moment. They are at an analytic advantage: they have heard—and not-heard—"this kind of thing" before.

Zerubavel (2019, 62) recommends that researchers be "alert to any possible sign of *hesitation*" (emphasis in the original). I can imagine an interview strategy of calling attention to such hesitations, as with "I noticed that you just hesitated." For encouraging research participants to speak about what is silenced societally, Sue and Robertson (2019, 83) suggest questions such as "Have you ever witnessed the silence being broken?" (on racism). Other possibilities are questions such as "What does that metaphor mean to you?" and "Why did you qualify your response in that way?"

To thrust unsaid into the open is to challenge the power positions that unsaid helps secure. I am not sure that is the job of the researcher, though I can imagine the pro argument. Certainly, such an intervention is a viable form of political resistance. Intervening in silence is performative, potentially exposing overlooked sites of deception by the powerful. It does occur to me that interventions in silence could provoke opposition in the same way that intervening in "speech" does. A reasonable reader might go on the alert: "First what I say and now what I *don't* say is policed!" Erstwhile appeals to free speech would be expanded as appeals to free communication, silence included.[6] It is useful to consider and plan for such collateral possibilities, including pushback.

In fact, what people do not say is already evaluated and policed a great deal. In courtrooms, "the witness who pauses before answering questions put to him or her is subject to negative inference about his or her veracity" (Walker 1985, 55). One invokes the statutory right to remain silent or to issue "no comment" at one's own peril: unsaid is often taken to mean something errant (Garbutt 2018). Silence in the present about information that surfaces later could be incriminating. Even beyond legal hearings—say, at a work meeting—one's silence may be taken for agreement with whatever is under discussion.

Unsaid analyses, formal and informal, are already underway and for a variety of helpful and harmful purposes. Figuring out tacit communication is part of ordinary sense-making, of determining what one must know to get along. What I aimed to provide in this book is a set of research strategies for doing unsaid inquiry well, by which I mean justly, intentionally, and legibly. I hope that methods of unsaid analysis will be further developed for the sake of better understanding harm-doing and harm-tolerating. I see much value in narrative criminologists demonstrating how unsaid in stories does, invites, and conceals harm. I hope that such research increases awareness, among both scholars and the public, of the discursive unsaid as a constitutive feature of harmful arrangements—that is to say, of how economies of expression work in conjunction with other economies to promote or hinder well-being.

A Word on Sampling

One of the first steps in any empirical analysis is to gather material to analyze. As I write this, the times have never been better for accessing textual data, given the availability of massive amounts of online comments, conversations, reports, and stories, and have never been worse for collecting primary data—talking to and interacting with participants—given fluctuating pandemic conditions and restrictions, including obstacles to travel and contact. Unsaid analysis is likely to proceed on any number of archived materials, even as ethnography is an invaluable source of information on missing subjects.

Unsaid analysis has implications for sample size. In general, qualitative research tends to involve samples (or corpuses, as they are called in linguistics) that are comparatively small. Scrutiny of the linguistic particulars of texts and the interactional nuances of communication, and a comparably effort-intensive ethnographic sensibility, will simply not allow the effective use of very large amounts of material. Probing and multifaceted as it is, unsaid analysis in particular demands manageable data sets. And yet, the unsaid analyst needs an amount of text large enough to grasp patterns, such as patterns of elaboration, where too little or too much is said. In other words, the more texts, the more variation one can think with and the more equipped one is to describe broad patterns. Arguably, broad patterns of textual exclusion are more socially impactful, so analysts are motivated to say something about them.

Longitudinal and cross-corpus comparisons may be used to pinpoint messages that are missing at some time and in some texts or outlets, and not others (Partington 2018).[1] Then, analysts can penetrate missing subjects—or "those not there"—as well as "those no longer there"—the social dynamism of going-missing (Ferrell 2018, 194). But a total or nearly total eclipse of discursive attention, or voids, such as nonhumans have suffered, is hard to discern synchronically or even diachronically. In that regard, I do have faith in comparisons of texts across groups, for example, comparison of narratives from persons with different ethical commitments (e.g., Presser, Schally, and Vossler 2020).

One's data set should contain, or should seem at the outset to contain, negative cases—ones that are poised to challenge the starting conjectures or, as the analysis proceeds, that seem to undermine the understandings one is so far developing. The researcher might launch the study with interesting, remarkable, and/or popular examples, but eventually supplement them with ones that are "not so obvious" or "tougher to crack." In this way the sample might grow, which weighs against an overly large starting sample.

Conversely, if the sample consists of primary interview data, then it might shrink along with attrition of research participants. I expect that unsaid analysis will mainly involve material that is already in hand, including news articles and online content. In such cases, the researcher more commonly faces an overabundance than a shortfall of data. The lucky researcher has just enough data to make solid observations but not too much to become overwhelmed and confused. An ideal situation is one in which the researcher has obtained all the text there is to obtain on an issue related to their scholarly goals.

It is up to the researcher to decide how many and which of the methodological foci outlined in this book they would target. More foci potentially allow one to tell a bigger and more complex story about unsaid. But more foci will generally demand more material. Again, working with less—fewer foci in this case—can enable deeper study. The social construction of one's findings has typically been ancillary to the "main" findings. So it may be with the social construction of absences, in which case the busy researcher can proceed without that dimension of unsaid. Or, the social construction of absences might get treated as an elementary object of attention, which I would take to signal the maturity of the field of unsaid inquiry within sociology.

Glossary

absence	The state of something being missing or inaccessible to sensory grasp.
ambiguous directive	A call to action that is vague so as to be implicit.
code word	A word that substitutes for some other word that is problematic, for example, it carries a negative evaluation.
cognitive dissonance	Psychic conflict due to holding contradictory ideas.
context	The circumstances surrounding and impinging on events, actions, and experiences.
conversation analysis	Close study of talk that goes on in contexts of ordinary interaction.
counter-hegemony	Opposition to ideological dominance.
criminology	Study of crime, including definitions of and responses to crime.
critical discourse analysis	Systematic analysis of texts that sustain unequal power.
cultural structure	A relatively stable social formation (e.g., idiom, narrative, or custom) that constructs meaning.

denial of injury | Denial that anyone is harmed by one's action; one neutralization technique identified by Sykes and Matza (1957).

denial of victim | Denial that an alleged victim is actually a victim; one neutralization technique identified by Sykes and Matza (1957).

dialectic | Productive relationship between contradictory phenomena.

discourse | Socially impactful system of knowledge that gets communicated.

dog whistle | Hostile communication that is strategically understated, often intended for supportive audiences.

domain analysis | Study of what *source domain* is applied to a *target domain* in metaphor and carrying what meanings; inspired by Lakoff and Johnson (1980).

elaboration | Textual content added for the sake of explanation.

epistemic | Having to do with knowledge and its validity.

erasure | Textual *exclusion*, usually intended.

exclusion | Omission of something or someone.

figuration | To make meaning through *figurative expression*.

figurative expression | Nonliteral expression such as metaphor or hyperbole.

harm | Trouble caused by another.

hedge | To reduce commitment to, and hence the impact of, a statement within a text, often by offering two incompatible perspectives.

hegemony | Ideological dominance.

ideology | An idea or claim that sustains power relations, often part of a constellation of ideas or claims.

interlocutor | A partner in communication.

intertextuality | Reference within a text to other texts.

master narrative | The dominant and dominating account of a phenomenon.

metaphor	A word or expression that refers to one thing, being, or concept in terms of a different thing, being, or concept.
metonymic storytelling	Narration that omits parts or events, often using concise conventional expressions for the omissions.
metonymy	An expression that refers to one thing, being, or concept in terms of a closely related thing, being, or concept.
missing subject	A relevant person, people, event, action, experience, context, or perspective excluded from a text.
narrative	An account of an experience of events over time that makes a point; see also *story*.
narrative criminology	Study of the influence of stories on harm.
nominalization	An expression that constructs a process as a thing.
normative	Socially standard and sanctioned.
overstatement	Statement containing seemingly unnecessary content.
perspective	A point of view.
power paradox	Discourse simultaneously avowing one's power and one's powerlessness vis-à-vis some action.
pragmatics	Linguistic subfield concerned with language in use.
presupposition	Meaning taken for granted in a text.
signified	Meaning intended to be conveyed via a *signifier*.
signifier	Material thing actually grasped or read, such as a word; the *signified* is the meaning one is meant to derive from the signifier.
silent stakes	A communicator's unspoken purposes in making a particular statement.
small story	Discursive form with limited narrativity; small stories may be allusions to stories, representations of events in progress, and references to stories not told.

source domain	Phenomenon (e.g., war) from which the meaning of a metaphor borrows; the concept is applied to some *target domain*.
speech act theory	Proposition that communication does things.
story	An account of an experience of events over time that makes a point; see also *narrative*. Note that many narratologists view story as the events and narrative as their discursive representation.
subaltern	Beings positioned as inferior or marginal.
subjugation	The state of being dominated.
target domain	Phenomenon (e.g., public policy) meant to be described by a *metaphor*.
text	A symbolic object that can be studied.
transitivity analysis	Analysis of discursive representations of people as acting or not-acting.
trope	Abbreviated text, even a single word, that alludes to stories.
understatement	Statement missing or only minimally addressing some key element or elements.
unsaid	Text that matters for the meaning of a statement but is absent to varying degrees.
void	Complete exclusion of something or some being from a text; see also *missing subject*.
zemiology	The study of harm, also known as the social harm perspective.

Notes

PREFACE

1. I define harm as trouble caused by another (Presser 2013). Harm presumes and is correlated with power: an agent of harm is one with the capacity to cause it.

2. Lacan (1977, 93) considered unsaid: "Certainly we must be attentive to the 'un-said' that lies in the holes of the discourse, but this does not mean that we are to listen as if to someone knocking on the other side of a wall." The question that motivated me to develop this book was: How are we to listen?

3. See Austin (1962), Berger and Luckmann (1967), Bourdieu (1991), Fairclough (1992), Foucault (1980), and Hall (2001).

CHAPTER 1. KEPT QUIET

1. Criminology is the study of crime, including the study of designations of some conduct as crime, the etiology of crime, and societal responses to crime. Critical criminologists, broadly speaking, emphasize the social construction of whatever gets called crime. Some critical criminologists and

other researchers have called for an alternative academic discipline focused on harm, known as zemiology.

2. This discussion is related to one of microaggressions, "brief, commonplace, often subtle verbal, behavioral, and environmental indignities" perpetrated against members of subaltern groups (Freeman and Stewart 2020, 37; see also Sue 2010). The microaggressive gestures add up to exclusion and repression.

3. The labeled sometimes proudly reclaim the label, thus defying the silencing.

4. Note, however that an individual, say a child sexual abuse survivor, may be forced to keep a secret. In this case someone else benefits from the silence. Choosing to be silent is surely not the same thing as being silenced.

5. I appreciate a poststructuralist conceptualization of text as "every meaningfully organized sign system" (Brockmeier 2002, 32), which includes oral, written, visual, and performative forms. This book and my method presently focus on written texts, however.

6. Potter and Wetherell (1987, 33) smartly observe: "To present yourself as a wonderful human being to someone, you perhaps should not say 'I am a wonderful human being', but you might modestly slip into the conversation at some 'natural' point that you work for charities, have won an academic prize, read Goethe, and so on."

7. Ultimate power belongs to the one whose name cannot be spoken. Examples include Voldemort in the Harry Potter book series and God in the Jewish religion.

8. Foucault (1978, 86) made a complementary point: "power is tolerable only on condition that it mask a substantial part of itself."

9. Even having been exposed to information, persons may be ignorant if they do not grasp or try to grasp its meaning (Dotson 2011). Hence, Berenstain (2020, 740) notes that "Black women often see the truth behind white men's oppressive actions in ways that white women choose not to" such as concerns sexual aggression.

10. Likewise, forgetting—losing or avoiding awareness of that which was once known—is collective (Nietzsche 1983).

11. Material objects, arrangements, images, and actions, including nonverbal gestures, also communicate and also do so through absences. I have given less thought to how unsaid analysis could apply in analyzing these (see Brockmeier's 2002 discussion of monuments). The things images "say" is rather its own issue: the images are "not said" by (narrow) definition.

12. Missing material is a key problematic of another subfield of linguistics, computational linguistics.

13. Grice (1975) more generally emphasizes speakers' intentions. Thomas (1995, 120) notes: "In pragmatics we are interested only in intentional indirectness." I am suggesting that unsaid analysis, like discourse analysis, does not share such an emphasis.

14. Fairclough (1992, 4), in setting out his "critical discourse analysis" framework, proposed that any discursive event has three dimensions: social practice, text, and discursive practice (see also Fairclough 2013, 94). Any discursive event should be read as all three things, he argues.

15. In fact, discursive forms, including reports, arguments, messages, and putative stories, may be described in terms of a continuum of narrativity, rather than as "a narrative" or "not a narrative" (Herman 2002). For simplicity, I will set aside this wisdom and treat texts as *either* narrative or not narrative.

16. Lyricism brings us to sensory arousal, which brings us to affect. Affect theorists generally emphasize the ineffability of embodied experience. Affective experience is not, they say, determined in the present, nor by what is said or not said. Affect theory would seem to have little to do with unsaid analysis, inasmuch as it eschews signification (Brown and Tucker 2010). Yet, if "embodied action" is understood as "bound up with talk" in some way, then talk's absences may be part of affect-theoretic inquiry (Wetherell 2013, 360).

17. The unsaid analysis that I am setting out is primarily interpretative. However, quantification has a place, such as in determining the amount of space that is allotted and the amount of space that should be allotted to persons, events, actions, experiences, contexts, and perspectives within some text (chapter 4).

CHAPTER 2. TOO LITTLE OR TOO MUCH SAID

1. Fuery (1995, 167–68) describes the matter as a practical one: "It must be acknowledged that distinguishing between intended absences and a repression of the signifier can be difficult, and in these cases there is something to be said for recognizing absence as the central edict rather than examining why it presides in text."

2. This strategy is a real-time analogue to comparing what was said with (past) unsaid that surfaces later: for example, old email communications.

3. Overstatement is not to be confused with what discourse analysts call overlexicalization, where "quasi-synonymous terms" are repeated throughout a text (Teo 2000). Overstatement need not entail repetition. Rather, it is indicated by seemingly unnecessary text.

4. Note that Haley's criticism of Trump's "asking" for an investigation excludes Trump's ambiguous threat of withholding aid.

5. It is quite possible that the communicator is not in any position *to* act. The point is not that communicators are "bad" or "wrong" for performing engagement, but simply that they do perform engagement.

6. See Presser (2018), chapter 5, for additional discussion of the story of antisociality.

7. That crime is a social construct is a fact, but one that many criminologists relegate to unsaid. Even critical criminologists seem reluctant to use the word *fact* in this regard.

8. Gottfredson and Hirschi (1990, 14) write: "Criminology once had an idea of crime, an idea it lost with the development of the scientific perspective."

CHAPTER 3. FIGURATIVE EXPRESSION

1. Other figurative devices exclude as well. Consider sarcasm (the true opinion is not explicated) and idioms such as "boys will be boys" (the characteristics under discussion are not stated).

2. See Davidson (1978) for a critical view, according to which the meaning behind metaphors is ultimately indeterminate.

3. One such database is the MetaNet Metaphor Wiki (https://metaphor .icsi.berkeley.edu/pub/en/index.php/Category:Metaphor), which includes 685 pages of metaphors in English at the time of this writing.

4. Ask: What is the emotional atmosphere like there? Is action urgent, or should we deliberate? Who and what has agency? Whose agency is constrained? Whose agency is denied?

5. I conducted interviews with 27 men in total in several states in the United States—following agency contacts—on the basis of the men's reporting having committed serious violence. The interviews were minimally structured around their lives and the violence they had perpetrated. This, my doctoral dissertation project, was oriented toward questions of how men who perpetrated violence constructed life stories and identities. I had not purposefully explored unsaid for that study.

6. Charged with rape, Tim was ultimately convicted of gross sexual imposition.

7. We returned to the interview after a short break, at which point I prompted Tim: "Um, you were saying—okay, so you were in [name of prison]—you'd gotten out of [name of prison] for breaking and ent—Was [name] a prison?" Tim replied as above.

8. Denial is nurtured by conspiracy theories according to which the pandemic has been faked or exaggerated (Lynas 2020).

9. It is entirely possible that the president was unaware of this fact, which raises the question of whether he was using the verb form "isolating" in regard to the virus figuratively. But figurative expression does not require an intent to communicate nonliterally.

10. Lo is a name I commonly go by.

11. A related concept is Aesopian language, which is likewise used to refer to coded communication, though it suggests more than a few words.

CHAPTER 4. MISSING SUBJECTS

1. By "individual" I mean to include humans and nonhumans. I do not mean to stress individuality over affiliation. Whereas a dominant perspective holds that only humans are persons, some philosophers have argued for the extension of personhood to nonhumans (Francione 2008). Other philosophers, like DeGrazia (2006), argue that too much is made of personhood and that nonpersons do not necessarily "have radically inferior moral status" (49). I will not say more on this debate but have in mind humans and nonhumans among persons, despite the challenges of learning the perspectives, concerns, and desires of members of the latter group.

2. Nominalizations construct processes as nouns: for example, "protesting" becomes "a protest." Kress and Hodge (1979) identify the erasures involved. For instance, "nominalizations are not marked for tense, so they are outside indications of time or modality," and "complex relations are collapsed into single entities" (27). Nominalizations disappear persons as well as actions, their intentions, and their dynamism.

3. See Kaiser Family Foundation (2022) on ultrasound laws and National Right to Life (n.d.) on the Child Interstate Abortion Notification Act and the Protecting Individuals with Down Syndrome Act.

4. I imagine Johnston here drawing subtle attention, through the use of scare quotes, to the intersecting meanings of "unremarkable"—figuratively as mundane, literally as unsayable.

5. Not to be minimized, however, is the problem of socially marginalized persons not receiving a hearing when they do tell their stories (Colvin 2017). Story reception varies with social position: "configurations of power and resources determine what kind of a hearing particular stories secure" (Polletta 2006, 167). Since voice and power are reciprocally constituted, there is hope for significant change by targeting either voice or power.

6. The literary concept of free indirect discourse describes a strategy of revealing a character's thoughts without marking them out as such. Without any explicit statement as to thoughts, for example, we grasp those of the character Carmen in Ann Patchett's 2001 novel, *Bel Canto*: "Would it be the worst thing in the world if nothing happened at all, if they all stayed together in this generous house? Carmen prayed hard" (156).

7. A much-debated question is whether one who desires some activity that does not serve their well-being is nonetheless a victim. In general, that which is called violence tends to occlude the voice and personhood of victims in both the event and its aftermath; as such, expressed desire (e.g., for BDSM activity) rules out the designation of the activity as violence.

8. Storytelling has also been cited for flattening views of life experience, promoting individually centered perspectives (Mäkelä 2018), and inculcating ideological worldviews (Fernandes 2017; Fox 1999; Zhang and Dong 2019). Strawson (2004) contends that too much concern with narrating experience can prevent one from experiencing the moment; he writes that narrativity "is in the sphere of ethics more of an affliction or a bad habit than a prerequisite of a good life" (450).

9. Excessive (as opposed to deficient) attention to certain persons, events, actions, experiences, contexts, and perspectives could be an alternative means of assessing missing subjects.

CHAPTER 5. THE SOCIAL CONSTRUCTION
OF ABSENCES

1. The influence of real and imagined interlocutors/audiences is broad. Literary scholars have paid considerable attention to the role of readers in making meaning of stories. Schools of thought centered on "transaction" and "reader response," following figures such as Wolfgang Iser (1972) and

Louise Rosenblatt (1978), contend that "one text is potentially capable of several different realizations, and no reading can ever exhaust the full potential, for each individual reader will fill in the gaps in his own way, thereby excluding the various other possibilities" (Iser 1972, 285). Similarly, Barthes (1977) famously proclaimed the "death of the Author," calling the text "a tissue of quotations drawn from the innumerable centres of culture" (146). Even if we can imagine a text prior to contact, "the author must more or less consciously create the image of the reader he is addressing" (Rosenblatt 1978, 76), and such influence extends beyond literary work to real-world communication.

2. The bill became law on March 28, 2022, and went into effect July 1 of that year.

3. The exchange can be viewed at https://www.youtube.com /watch?v=JIjenjANqAk.

4. This particular unsaid—concerning the menace of Arabs—is bipartisan, and deeply rooted in contemporary Western societies. Concerning Barack Obama, a journalist wrote in June 2008: "The candidate has vigorously denied a false, viral rumor that he himself is Muslim. The denials at times seem to imply to some that there is something wrong with the faith, though Obama occasionally adds that he means no disrespect to Islam" (Smith 2008).

5. Alternatively, McCain's response can be conceived as "within-frame negation" (as opposed to "cross-frame negation") following a presupposed framing of Arabs as untrustworthy (Polyzou 2015, 131).

CHAPTER 6. CONCLUDING REMARKS: BOUNDLESS TEXTS, BETTER WORLDS

1. Titscher et al. (2012, 164) put it well: "Critical discourse analysis must be intelligible in its interpretations and explanations. The way in which investigators have arrived at their results must be recognizable."

2. Within criminology, Hallsworth and Young (2008, 132), highlighting the central role of silence in crime, take this encompassing view of the unsaid: "we need to focus . . . on the production of social worlds where things that ought to be said never are, where voices that should speak are silenced and where those with the power to speak, say nothing." Linguist Stibbe (2015, 144) distinguishes three categories of "erasure": the void, "where 'something important' is completely excluded from a text"; the

mask, "where it is erased but replaced by a distorted version of itself"; and the trace, "where something is partially erased but still present."

3. Actually, the reader-response-theoretic position is far stronger. A guiding light is Fish's (1980, 3) famous statement, "The reader's response is not *to* the meaning; it is the meaning."

4. Questions of whether Trump intended to provoke imminent violence with his words are distinguishable ones that I will not take up here (Nossel 2021).

5. Action research and participant-observation studies stand in marked contrast.

6. *Free speech* is itself an idiom that conceals unsaid commitments, for example, ideological presuppositions about what freedom is (e.g., an individual holding) and who its beneficiaries are (e.g., everyone equally).

APPENDIX

1. Useful examples are available in the volume edited by Schröter and Taylor (2018).

References

Abbott, H. Porter. 2002. *The Cambridge Introduction to Narrative.* Cambridge University Press.

———. 2013. *Real Mysteries: Narrative and the Unknowable.* Ohio State University Press.

ABC11.com. 2021. "'Really Bad Day': Sheriff Spokesperson Criticized for Minimizing Alleged Georgia Gunman's Deadly Rampage." *ABC11 Eyewitness News,* March 18. https://abc11.com/atlanta-spa-shooting-jay-baker-bad-day-cherokee-county-sheriff/10426441/.

Achenbach, Joel. 2020. "Shutdowns Prevented 60 Million Coronavirus Infections in the U.S., Study Finds." *Washington Post,* June 8. https://www.washingtonpost.com/health/2020/06/08/shutdowns-prevented-60-million-coronavirus-infections-us-study-finds/.

Agozino, Biko. 2003. *Counter-Colonial Criminology: A Critique of Imperialist Reason.* London: Pluto Press.

Ahmed, Sara. 2006. "The Nonperformativity of Antiracism." *Meridians: Feminism, Race, Transnationalism* 7(1): 104–26.

Alcántara-Plá, Manuel, and Ana Ruiz-Sánchez. 2018. "Not for Twitter: Migration as a Silenced Topic in the 2015 Spanish General Election." In *Exploring Silence and Absence in Discourse: Empirical Approaches,* edited by Melani Schröter and Charlotte Taylor, 25–64. Cham, Switzerland: Palgrave Macmillan.

Alexander, Jeffrey, and Philip Smith. 2002. "The Strong Program in Cultural Sociology: Elements of a Structural Hermeneutics." In *Handbook of Sociological Theory*, edited by Jonathan H. Turner, 135–50. New York: Kluwer/Plenum.

Allen, Graham. 2011. *Intertextuality*, 2nd ed. London: Routledge.

Althusser, Louis. 1971. "Ideology, and Ideological State Apparatuses (Notes towards an Investigation)." In Lenin and Philosophy and Other Essays, translated by Ben Brewster, 127–86. New York: Monthly Review Press.

Amnesty International. 2018. "Key Facts about the Migrant and Refugee Caravans Making Their Way to the USA," November 16. https://www.amnesty.org/en/latest/news/2018/11/key-facts-about-the-migrant-and-refugee-caravans-making-their-way-to-the-usa/.

Andrews, Molly. 2004. "Opening to the Original Contributions: Counter-Narratives and the Power to Oppose." In *Considering Counter-Narratives: Narrating, Resisting, Making Sense*, edited by Michael Bamberg and Molly Andrews, 1–6. Amsterdam: John Benjamins.

Atkinson, J. Maxwell, and Paul Drew. 1979. *Order in Court: The Organization of Verbal Interaction in Judicial Settings*. Atlantic Highlands, NJ: Humanities Press.

Austin, J. L. 1962. *How to Do Things with Words*. Harvard University Press.

Baker, Peter, and Katie Rogers. 2018. "In Trump's America, the Conversation Turns Ugly and Angry, Starting at the Top." *New York Times,* June 20. https://www.nytimes.com/2018/06/20/us/politics/trump-language-immigration.html.

Baldwin, James. 1976. *The Devil Finds Work*. London: Michael Joseph.

Bamberg, Michael, and Molly Andrews, eds. 2004. *Considering Counter-Narratives: Narrating, Resisting, Making Sense*. Amsterdam: John Benjamins.

Bamberg, Michael, and Alexandra Georgakopoulou. 2008. "Small Stories as a New Perspective in Narrative and Identity Analysis." *Text & Talk* 28(3): 377–96.

Barnet, Belinda. 2003. "The Erasure of Technology in Cultural Critique." *Fibreculture Journal* 1. https://one.fibreculturejournal.org/fcj-005-the-erasure-of-technology-in-cultural-critique.

Bar-On, Dan. 1999. *The Indescribable and the Undiscussable: Reconstructing Human Discourse after Trauma.* Central European University Press.

Barrera, Dan Jerome. 2017. "Drug War Stories and the Philippine President." *Asian Journal of Criminology* 12(4): 341–59.

Barthes, Roland. 1957. *Mythologies,* translated by Annette Lavers. New York: Hill and Wang.

———. 1977. *Image, Music, Text,* translated by Steven Heath. London: Fontana.

Bauder, David. 2018. "News Media Hesitate to Use 'Lie' for Trump's Misstatements." Associated Press, August 29. https://apnews.com/article/88675d3fdd674c7c9ec70f170f6e4a1a.

Bell, Lee Anne. 2003. "Telling Tales: What Stories Can Teach Us about Racism." *Race Ethnicity and Education* 6(1): 3–28.

Beneke, Timothy. 1982. *Men on Rape.* New York: St. Martin's Press.

Bengtsson, Tea Torbenfeldt, and Lars Fynbo. 2018. "Analysing the Significance of Silence in Qualitative Interviewing: Questioning and Shifting Power Relations." *Qualitative Research* 18(1): 19–35.

Berenstain, Nora. 2020. "White Feminist Gaslighting." *Hypatia* 35(4): 733–58.

Berger, Peter, and Thomas Luckmann. 1967. *The Social Construction of Reality: A Treatise in the Sociology of Knowledge.* New York: Anchor Books.

Bhattacharya, Himika. 2009. "Performing Silence: Gender, Violence, and Resistance in Women's Narratives from Lahaul, India." *Qualitative Inquiry* 15(2): 359–71.

Billig, Michael, and Cristina Marinho. 2019. "Literal and Metaphorical Silences in Rhetoric: Examples from the Celebration of the 1974 Revolution in the Portuguese Parliament." In *Qualitative Studies of Silence: The Unsaid as Social Action,* edited by Amy Jo Murray and Kevin Durrheim, 21–37. Cambridge University Press.

Bilmes, Jack. 2009. "Constituting Silence: Life in the World of Total Meaning." *Semiotica* 98(1–2): 73–87.

Blake, Aaron. 2019. "7 Takeaways from the Rough Transcript of Trump's Call with Ukraine's President." *Washington Post,* September 25. https://www.washingtonpost.com/politics/2019/09/25/takeaways-transcript-trumps-call-with-ukraines-president/.

———. 2020. "Trump Flirts with a Less-Aggressive Coronavirus Response, Echoing Fox News." *Washington Post,* March 23. https://

www.washingtonpost.com/politics/2020/03/23/trump-flirts-with-less-aggressive-coronavirus-response-echoing-fox-news/.

———. 2021. "Four Final Takeaways from Trump's Impeachment Trial." *Washington Post,* February 13. https://www.washingtonpost.com/politics/2021/02/13/takeaways-trump-impeachment-trial-final/.

Blanco, María Del Pilar, and Esther Peeren, eds. 2013. *The Spectralities Reader: Ghosts and Haunting in Contemporary Cultural Theory.* New York: Bloomsbury.

Blix, Bodil H., Vera Caine, D. Jean Clandinin, and Charlotte Berendonk. 2021. "Considering Silences in Narrative Inquiry: An Intergenerational Story of a Sami Family." *Journal of Contemporary Ethnography,* https://doi.org/10.1177/08912416211003145.

Blumenthal, Paul. 2020. "Donald Trump Wants to Fight Coronavirus as a 'Wartime President.' He Can't." *Huffington Post,* April 14. https://www.huffpost.com/entry/donald-trump-coronavirus-war_n_5e95b36cc5b636ad1077f0f4.

Bourdieu, Pierre. 1991. *Language and Symbolic Power,* edited by John Thompson and translated by Gino Raymond and Matthew Adamson. Cambridge: Polity Press.

Briggs, Daniel, and Rubén Monge Gamero. 2017. *Dead-End Lives: Drugs and Violence in the City Shadows.* Bristol, UK: Policy Press.

Brisman, Avi. 2019. "Stories of Environmental Crime, Harm and Protection: Narrative Criminology and Green Cultural Criminology." In *The Emerald Handbook of Narrative Criminology,* edited by Jennifer Fleetwood, Lois Presser, Sveinung Sandberg, and Thomas Ugelvik, 153–72. Bingley, UK: Emerald.

Brockmeier, Jens. 2002. "Remembering and Forgetting: Narrative as Cultural Memory." *Culture & Psychology* 8(1): 15–43.

———. 2004. "What Makes a Story Coherent?" In *Communication and Metacommunication in Human Development,* edited by Angela Uchoa Branco and Jaan Valsiner, 285–306. Charlotte, NC: Information Age.

Brown, Steven D., and Ian Tucker. 2010. "Eff the Ineffable: Affect, Somatic Management, and Mental Health Service Users." In *The Affect Theory Reader,* edited by Melissa Gregg and Gregory J. Seigworth, 229–49. Duke University Press.

Bruner, Jerome. 1986. *Actual Minds, Possible Worlds.* Harvard University Press.

———. 1990. *Acts of Meaning.* Harvard University Press.

Brunsma, David L., Eric S. Brown, and Peggy Placier. 2012. "Teaching Race at Historically White Colleges and Universities: Identifying and Dismantling the Walls of Whiteness." *Critical Sociology* 39(5): 717–38.

Bunch, Will. 2020. "No, President Trump, You Can't Bomb a Virus. We Need Expertise and Empathy—Not a War." *Philadelphia Inquirer,* April 2. https://www.inquirer.com/health/coronavirus/coronavirus-covid-trump-war-president-military-ventilators-20200402.html.

Burt, Martha R. 1980. "Cultural Myths and Supports for Rape." *Journal of Personality and Social Psychology* 38(2): 217–30.

Butalia, Urvashi. 2000. *The Other Side of Silence: Voices from the Partition of India.* Duke University Press.

Butler, Judith. 2004. *Precarious Life: The Powers of Mourning and Violence.* London: Verso.

Canadian Resource Centre for Victims of Crime. 2007. "Brief to the Standing Committee on Access to Information, Privacy and Ethics." http://crcvc.ca/docs/PIPEDA.BRIEF.pdf.

Caracciolo, Marco. 2012. "On the Experientiality of Stories: A Follow-Up on David Herman's 'Narrative Theory and the Intentional Stance'." *Partial Answers: Journal of Literature and the History of Ideas* 10(2): 197–221.

Carter, Rodney G. S. 2006. "Of Things Said and Unsaid: Power, Archival Silences, and Power in Silence." *Archivaria* 61: 215–33.

Cathey, Libby, and Jack Arnholz. 2020. "Coronavirus Government Response Updates: 'Biggest Decision of My Life', Trump Says, about Reopening Country." *ABC News,* April 11. https://abcnews.go.com/Politics/coronavirus-government-response-updates-trump-americans-back-work/story?id=70083632.

Chandler, Prentice, and Douglas McKnight. 2009. "The Failure of Social Education in the United States: A Critique of Teaching the National Story from 'White' Colourblind Eyes." *Journal for Critical Education Policy Studies* 7(2): 217–48.

Charmaz, Kathy. 2002. "Stories and Silences: Disclosures and Self in Chronic Illness." *Qualitative Inquiry* 8(3): 302–28.

Chatman, Seymour. 1978. *Story and Discourse: Narrative Structure in Fiction and Film.* Cornell University Press.

Christian, Barbara. 1985. *Black Feminist Criticism: Perspectives on Black Women Writers.* New York: Pergamon Press.

Christie, Nils. 1977. "Conflicts as Property." *British Journal of Criminology* 17(1): 1–15.

Clifton, Jonathan, and Dorien Van De Mieroop. 2016. *Master Narratives, Identities, and the Stories of Former Slaves*. Amsterdam: John Benjamins.

Colvin, Sarah. 2017. *"Unerhört?* Prisoner Narratives as Unlistened-to Stories (and Some Reflections on the Picaresque)." *Modern Language Review* 112(2): 440–58.

Cohen, Stanley. 2001. *States of Denial: Knowing about Atrocities and Suffering*. Cambridge: Polity Press.

Cohn, Carol. 1987. "Sex and Death in the Rational World of Defense Intellectuals." *Signs: Journal of Women in Culture and Society* 12(4): 687–718.

ConsiderVeganism.com. 2019. "Animal Kill Counter." http://consider veganism.com/counter/.

Cook, Noble David. 1998. *Born to Die: Disease and Conquest, 1492–1650*. Cambridge University Press.

Copes, Heith, Andy Hochstetler, and Sveinung Sandberg. 2015. "Using a Narrative Framework to Understand the Drugs and Violence Nexus." *Criminal Justice Review* 4(1): 32–46.

Cox, Alexandra. 2017. *Trapped in a Vice: The Consequences of Confinement for Young People*. Rutgers University Press.

Crouse, Lindsay. 2021. "Naomi Osaka and the Power of Nope." *New York Times*, June 1. https://www.nytimes.com/2021/06/01/opinion/naomi-osaka-french-open-tennis.html.

Das, Veena, and Ashis Nandy. 1985. "Violence, Victimhood, and the Language of Silence." *Contributions to Indian Sociology* 19(1): 177–95.

Davidson, Donald. 1978. "What Metaphors Mean." *Critical Inquiry* 5(1): 31–47.

Davies, Bronwyn, and Rom Harré. 1990. "Positioning: The Discursive Production of Selves." *Journal for the Theory of Social Behavior* 20(1): 43–63.

De Fina, Anna. 2009. "Narratives in Interview: The Case of Accounts." *Narrative Inquiry* 19(2): 233–58.

De Fina, Anna, and Alexandra Georgakopoulou. 2012. *Analyzing Narrative Discourse and Sociolinguistic Perspectives*. Cambridge University Press.

DeGrazia, David. 2006. "On the Question of Personhood beyond *Homo Sapiens*." In *In Defense of Animals: The Second Wave*, edited by Peter Singer, 40–53. Malden, MA: Blackwell.

Delmas, Magali A., and Vanessa Cuerel Burbano. 2011. "The Drivers of Greenwashing." *California Management Review* 54(1): 64–87.

deMause, Neil. 2020. "Top 16 Euphemisms US Headline Writers Used for Police Beating the Shit out of People." Fairness and Accuracy in Reporting, June 7. https://fair.org/home/top-16-euphemisms-us-headline-writers-used-for-police-beating-the-shit-out-of-people/.

Dotson, Kristie. 2011. "Tracking Epistemic Violence, Tracking Practices of Silencing." *Hypatia* 26(2): 236–57.

Dove.com. n.d. #BeautyBias. https://www.dove.com/us/en/stories/campaigns/-beautybias.html.

Drew, Paul. 2018. "The Interface between Pragmatics and Conversation Analysis." In *Pragmatics and Its Interfaces,* edited by Cornelia Illie and Neil R. Norrick, 59–84. Amsterdam: John Benjamins.

Durrani, Sameera. 2018. "Absence in Visual Narratives: The Story of Iran and Pakistan across Time." In *Exploring Silence and Absence in Discourse: Empirical Approaches,* edited by Melani Schröter and Charlotte Taylor, 65–93. Cham, Switzerland: Palgrave Macmillan.

Eagleton, Terry. 1991. *Ideology: An Introduction.* London: Verso.

Edbauer, Jenny. 2005. "Unframing Models of Public Distribution: From Rhetorical Situation to Rhetorical Ecologies." *Rhetoric Society Quarterly* 35(4): 5–24.

Eisenberg, Eric. 1984. "Ambiguity as Strategy in Organizational Communication." *Communication Monographs* 51(3): 227–42.

Entman, Robert M. 1993. "Framing: Toward Clarification of a Fractured Paradigm." *Journal of Communication* 43(4): 51–58.

Ewick, Patricia, and Susan Silbey. 1995. "Subversive Stories and Hegemonic Tales: Towards a Sociology of Narrative." *Law & Society Review* 29(1): 197–228.

Fairclough, Norman. 1989. *Language and Power.* New York: Longman.

———. 1992. *Discourse and Social Change.* Cambridge: Polity Press.

———. 2013. *Critical Discourse Analysis: The Critical Study of Language,* 2nd ed. London: Routledge.

Ferber, Abby L. 2007. "Whiteness Studies and the Erasure of Gender." *Sociology Compass* 1(1): 265–82.

Fernandes, Sujatha. 2017. *Curated Stories: The Uses and Misuses of Storytelling.* Oxford University Press.

Féron, Élise. 2018. *Wartime Sexual Violence against Men: Masculinities and Power in Conflict Zones.* London: Rowman & Littlefield.

Ferreira, Victor S., L. Robert Slevc, and Erin S. Rogers. 2005. "How Do Speakers Avoid Ambiguous Linguistic Expressions?" *Cognition* 96(3): 263–84.

Ferrell, Jeff. 2018. *Drift: Illicit Mobility and Uncertain Knowledge.* University of California Press.

Festinger, Leon. 1957. *A Theory of Cognitive Dissonance.* Stanford University Press.

Filipovic, Jill. 2021. "Conservatives Say They Want to Help 'Parents' Stay Home. They Mean Mothers." *Washington Post,* May 3. https:// www.washingtonpost.com/outlook/2021/05/03/conservatives-childcare -parents-mothers/.

Finkelstein, Avram. 2018. *After Silence: A History of AIDS through Its Images.* University of California Press.

Fish, Stanley. 1980. *Is There a Text in This Class? The Authority of Interpretive Communities.* Harvard University Press.

Fisher, Mark. 2014. *Ghosts of My Life: Writings on Depression, Hauntology and Lost Futures.* Alresford, Hants, UK: Zero Books.

Fivush, Robyn, and Monisha Pasupathi. 2019. "Silencing Self and Other through Autobiographical Narratives." In *Qualitative Studies of Silence: The Unsaid as Social Action,* edited by Amy Jo Murray and Kevin Durrheim, 126–46. Cambridge University Press.

Fleetwood, Jennifer. 2019. "Everyday Self-Defence: Hollaback Narratives, Habitus and Resisting Street Harassment." *British Journal of Sociology* 70(5):1709–29.

Florida House of Representatives. 2022. "CS/CS/HB 1557: Parental Rights in Education." https://www.myfloridahouse.gov/Sections/Bills /billsdetail.aspx?BillId=76545.

Fludernik, Monika. 1996. *Towards a "Natural" Narratology.* New York: Routledge.

Foucault, Michel. 1978. *The History of Sexuality,* Vol. 1, translated by Robert Hurley. New York: Pantheon.

———. 1980. *Power/Knowledge: Selected Interviews and Other Writings, 1972–1977.* Brighton: Harvester.

Fox, Kathryn J. 1999. "Changing Violent Minds: Discursive Correction and Resistance in the Cognitive Treatment of Violent Offenders in Prison." *Social Problems* 46: 88–103.

Francione, Gary L. 2008. *Animals as Persons: Essays on the Abolition of Animal Exploitation.* Columbia University Press.

Frank, Arthur W. 1995. *The Wounded Storyteller: Body, Illness, and Ethics.* University of Chicago Press.

———. 2010. *Letting Stories Breathe: A Socio-Narratology*. University of Chicago Press.

Freeman, Lauren, and Heather Stewart. 2020. "Sticks and Stones Can Break Your bones and Words Can Really Hurt You: A Standpoint Epistemological Reply to Critics of the Microaggression Research Program." In *Microaggressions and Philosophy*, edited by Lauren Freeman and Jeanine Weekes Schroer, 36–66. New York: Routledge.

Freeman, Mark. 2002. "The Presence of What is Missing: Memory, Poetry, and the Ride Home." In *Between Fathers and Sons: Critical Incident Narratives in the Development of Men's Lives*, edited by Robert J. Pellegrini and Theodore R. Sarbin, 165–76. New York: Haworth Clinical Practice Press.

Fuchs, Michael H. 2019. "Trump Is Using the Autocrat's Playbook. Democratic Institutions Must Step Up." *The Guardian*, October 17. https://www.theguardian.com/commentisfree/2019/oct/17/trump-autocrat-congress-judiciary-democracy.

Fuery, Patrick. 1995. *The Theory of Absence: Subjectivity, Signification and Desire*. Westport, CT: Greenwood Press.

Gair, Susan, and Sharon Moloney. 2013. "Unspeakable Stories: When Counter Narratives Are Deemed Unacceptable." *Qualitative Research Journal* 13(1): 49–61.

Garbutt, Joanna. 2018. "The Use of No Comment by Suspects in Police Interviews." In *Exploring Silence and Absence in Discourse: Empirical Approaches*, edited by Melani Schröter and Charlotte Taylor, 329–57. Cham, Switzerland: Palgrave Macmillan.

Garcia-Navarro, Lulu, Thomas L. Friedman, Ross Douthat, and Farah Stockman. 2022. "Four Opinion Writers on Ukraine: 'If This War Drags On, We Are in a Completely New World'." *New York Times*, March 24. https://www.nytimes.com/2022/03/24/opinion/ukraine-refugees-russia-war.html.

Gathings, M. J., and Kylie Parrotta. 2013. "The Use of Gendered Narratives in the Courtroom: Constructing an Identity Worthy of Leniency." *Journal of Contemporary Ethnography* 42(6): 668–89.

Gay, Roxane. 2018. *Not That Bad: Dispatches from Rape Culture*. New York: HarperCollins.

Genette, Gérard. 1980. *Narrative Discourse: An Essay in Method*, translated by Jane E. Lewin. Cornell University Press.

Gibbs, Raymond W., Jr. 1999. "Speaking and Thinking with Metonymy." In *Metonymy in Language and Thought*, edited by

Klaus-Uwe Panther and Günter Radden, 61–76. Amsterdam: John Benjamins.

Ginio, Ruth. 2010. "African Silences: Negotiating the Story of France's Colonial Soldiers, 1914-2009." In *Shadows of War: A Social History of Silence in the Twentieth Century,* edited by Efrat Ben-Ze'ev, Ruth Ginio, and Jay Winter, 138–52. Cambridge University Press.

Giora, Rachel. 1999. "On the Priority of Salient Meanings: Studies of Literal and Figurative Language." *Journal of Pragmatics* 31: 919–29.

Givhan, Robin. 2020. "George Floyd's Brother Came to Washington to Speak. But His Power Was in the Silences." *Washington Post,* June 11. https://www.washingtonpost.com/lifestyle/2020/06/10/philonise-floyd-george-brother-congress/.

Goatly, Andrew. 2007. *Washing the Brain: Metaphor and Hidden Ideology.* Amsterdam: John Benjamins.

Godart, Caroline. 2016. "Silence and Sexual Difference: Reading Silence in Luce Irigaray." *DiGeSt. Journal of Diversity and Gender Studies* 3(2): 9–22.

Goffman, Erving. 1955. "On Face-Work: An Analysis of Ritual Elements in Social Interaction." *Psychiatry* 18(3): 213–31.

———. 1959. *The Presentation of Self in Everyday Life.* New York: Anchor Books.

———. 1974. *Frame Analysis: An Essay on the Organization of the Experience.* New York: Harper & Row.

Gordon, Avery F. 1997. *Ghostly Matters: Haunting and the Sociological Imagination.* University of Minnesota Press.

Gottfredson, Michael R., and Travis Hirschi. 1990. *A General Theory of Crime.* Stanford University Press.

Graesser, Arthur C., Brent Olde, and Bianca Klettke. 2002. "How Does the Mind Construct and Represent Stories?" In *Narrative Impact: Social and Cognitive Foundations,* edited by Melanie C. Green, Jeffrey J. Strange, and Timothy C. Brock, 229–62. Mahwah, NJ: Lawrence Erlbaum.

Grice, H. Paul. 1975. "Logic and Conversation." In *Syntax and Semantics,* Vol. 3: *Speech Acts,* edited by Peter Cole and Jerry L. Morgan, 41–58. New York: Academic Press.

Gross, Matthias, and Linsey McGoey. 2015. "Introduction." In *Routledge International Handbook of Ignorance Studies,* edited by Matthias Gross and Linsey McGoey, 1–14. London: Routledge.

Guardian, The. 2016. "Philippines President Rodrigo Duterte Urges People to Kill Drug Addicts," July 1. https://www.theguardian.com

/world/2016/jul/01/philippines-president-rodrigo-duterte-urges-
people-to-kill-drug-addicts.

Gubrium, Jaber F., and James A. Holstein. 2009. *Analyzing Narrative Reality.* Los Angeles: SAGE.

Gullette, Margaret Morganroth. 2017. *Ending Ageism, or How Not to Shoot Old People.* Rutgers University Press.

Haaretz and Reuters. 2018. "Timeline: 560,000 Killed in Syria's War according to Updated Death Toll," December 10. https://www.haaretz .com/middle-east-news/syria/560-000-killed-in-syria-s-war-accord-ing-to-updated-death-toll-1.6700244.

Hadi, Atefeh. 2013. "A Critical Appraisal of Grice's Cooperative Principle." *Open Journal of Modern Linguistics* 3(1): 69–72.

Hagopian, Amy, Abraham D. Flaxman, Tim K. Takaro, Sahar A. Esa Al Shatari, Julie Rajaratnam, Stan Becker, Alison Levin-Rector, Lindsay Galway, Berq J. Hadi Al-Yasseri, William M. Weiss, Christopher J. Murray, and Gilbert Burnham. 2013. "Mortality in Iraq Associated with the 2003–2011 War and Occupation: Findings from a National Cluster Sample Survey by the University Collaborative Iraq Mortality Study." *PLoS Medicine,* October 15. https://doi.org/10.1371/journal .pmed.1001533.

Hall, Stuart. 2001. "Foucault: Power, Knowledge and Discourse." In *Discourse Theory and Practice: A Reader,* edited by Margaret Wetherell, Stephanie Taylor, and Simeon J. Yates, 72–81. London: SAGE.

Halliday, M. A. K. 1994. *Introduction to Functional Grammar,* 2nd ed. London: Edward Arnold.

Hallsworth, Simon, and Tara Young. 2008. "Crime and Silence: 'Death and Life Are in the Power of the Tongue' (Proverbs 18:21)." *Theoretical Criminology* 12(2): 131–52.

Halverson, Jeffry R., Goodall, H. L., Jr., and Steven R. Corman. 2011. *Master Narratives of Islamist Extremism.* New York: Palgrave Macmillan.

Hardy, Cynthia, Bill Harley, and Nelson Phillips. 2004. "Discourse Analysis and Content Analysis: Two Solitudes?" *Qualitative Methods* 2(1): 19–22.

Hedges, Chris. 2003. *What Every Person Should Know about War.* New York: Free Press.

Hedges, Elaine, and Shelley Fishkin, eds. 1994. *Listening to Silences: New Essays in Feminist Criticism.* Oxford University Press.

Heritage, John. 1984. *Garfinkel and Ethnomethodology.* Cambridge: Polity Press.

Herman, David. 1995. *Universal Grammar and Narrative Form.* Duke University Press.

———. 2002. *Story Logic: Problems and Possibilities of Narrative.* University of Nebraska Press.

———. 2009. *Basic Elements of Narrative.* West Sussex, UK: Wiley-Blackwell.

Herman, Judith Lewis. 1997. *Trauma and Recovery.* New York: Basic Books.

Hjelmgaard, Kim. 2020. "Iceland Has Tested More of Its Population for Coronavirus than Anywhere Else. Here's What It Learned." *USA Today,* April 10. https://eu.usatoday.com/story/news/world/2020/04/10/coronavirus-covid-19-small-nations-iceland-big-data/2959797001/.

Hoare, Quintin, and Geoffrey Nowell Smith, eds. and trans. 1996. *Selections from the Prison Notebooks of Antonio Gramsci.* London: Lawrence and Wishart.

Hoggan, James. 2019. *I'm Right and You're an Idiot: The Toxic State of Public Discourse and How to Clean It Up,* 2nd ed. Gabriola Island, BC, Canada: New Society.

Holstein, James A., and Jaber F. Gubrium. 2000. *The Self We Live By: Narrative Identity in a Postmodern World.* Oxford University Press.

hooks, bell. 1981. *Ain't I a Woman: Black Women and Feminism.* Boston, MA: South End Press.

Houston, Marsha, and Cheris Kramarae. 1991. "Speaking from Silence: Methods of Silencing and of Resistance." *Discourse & Society* 2(4): 387–99.

Huckin, Thomas. 2002. "Textual Silence and the Discourse of Homelessness." *Discourse & Society* 13(3): 347–72.

Hyvärinen, Matti. 2021. "Toward a Theory of Counter-Narratives." In *The Routledge Handbook of Counter-Narratives,* edited by Klarissa Lueg and Marianne Lundholt, 17–29. Abingdon, Oxon: Routledge.

Ingraham, Christopher. 2014. "We've Killed Off Half the World's Animals since 1970." *Washington Post,* September 30. https://www.washingtonpost.com/news/wonk/wp/2014/09/30/weve-killed-off-half-the-worlds-animals-since-1970/.

International Labour Office. 2017. *Global Estimates of Modern Slavery: Forced Labour and Forced Marriage.* Geneva. https://www.ilo.org/wcmsp5/groups/public/---dgreports/---dcomm/documents/publication/wcms_575479.pdf.

Iser, Wolfgang. 1972. "The Reading Process: A Phenomenological Approach." *New Literary History* 3(2): 279–99.

Jalbert, Paul L. 1994. "Structures of the 'Unsaid'." *Theory, Culture & Society* 11: 127–60.

Jaworski, Adam. 1993. *The Power of Silence: Social and Pragmatic Perspectives.* Newbury Park, CA: SAGE.

———, ed. 1997. *Silence: Interdisciplinary Perspectives.* Berlin: Mouton de Gruyter.

Jewell, Britta L., and Nicholas P. Jewell. 2020. "Opinion: The Huge Cost of Waiting to Contain the Pandemic." *New York Times,* April 14. https://www.nytimes.com/2020/04/14/opinion/covid-social-distancing.html.

Johnston, Alex. 2021. "Telling Something Else: Documentary beyond (Hi) story." *World Records Journal* 5(3). https://vols.worldrecordsjournal.org /05/03.

Joosse, Paul, Sandra Bucerius, and Sara K. Thompson. 2015. "Narratives and Counternarratives: Somali-Canadians on Recruitment as Foreign Fighters to Al- Shabaab." *British Journal of Criminology* 55(4): 811–32.

Kaiser Family Foundation. 2022. "State Ultrasound Requirements in Abortion Procedure." https://www.kff.org/womens-health-policy/state-indicator/ultrasound-requirements/.

Kangun, Norman, Les Carlson, and Stephen J. Grove. 1991. "Environmental Advertising Claims: A Preliminary Investigation." *Journal of Public Policy and Marketing* 10(2): 47–58.

Kärki, Kaisa. 2018. "Not Doings as Resistance." *Philosophy of the Social Sciences* 48(4): 364–84.

Karni, Annie, and Maggie Haberman. 2019. "After Keeping a Careful Distance from Trump, Nikki Haley Is All In." *New York Times,* November 19. https://www.nytimes.com/2019/11/19/us/politics/nikki-haley-trump.html.

Kellogg's. n.d. "Plant Protein." https://www.kelloggs.com/en_US/brands /morningstar-farms-consumer-brand.html.

Kendi, Ibram X. 2019. *How to Be an Antiracist.* New York: One World.

Kermode, Frank. 2000. *The Sense of an Ending: Studies in the Theory of Fiction.* Oxford University Press.

Kimmel, Michael S., and Matthew Mahler. 2003. "Adolescent Masculinity, Homophobia, and Violence: Random School Shootings 1982-2001." *American Behavioral Scientist* 46(10): 1439–58.

Kitzinger, Celia. 2000. "Doing Feminist Conversation Analysis." *Feminism & Psychology* 10(2): 163–93.

Koskela, Merja. 2013. "Same, Same but Different: Intertexual and Interdiscursive Features of Communication Strategy Texts." Discourse & Communication 7(4): 389–407.

Kress, Gunther, and Robert Hodge. 1979. Language as Ideology. London: Routledge & Kegan Paul.

Kurtz, Don L., and Lindsey Upton. 2017. "War Stories and Occupying Soldiers: A Narrative Approach to Understanding Police Culture and Community Conflict." *Critical Criminology* 25(4): 539–58.

Kurzon, Dennis. 1998. *Discourse of Silence*. John Benjamins: Amsterdam.

———. 2007. "Towards a Typology of Silence." *Journal of Pragmatics* 39: 1673–88.

La Ganga, Maria L. 2016. "The First Lady Who Looked Away: Nancy and the Reagans' Troubling AIDS Legacy." *The Guardian,* March 11. https://www.theguardian.com/us-news/2016/mar/11/nancy-ronald-reagan-aids-crisis-first-lady-legacy.

Labov, William, and Joshua Waletzky. 1967. "Narrative Analysis: Oral Versions of Personal Experience." In *Essays on the Verbal and Visual Arts,* edited by June Helms, 12–44. University of Washington Press.

Lacan, Jacques. 1977. "The Function and Field of Speech and Language in Psychoanalysis." In *Écrits: A Selection*, translated by Alan Sheridan, 30–113. New York: Norton.

Lakoff, George. 1993. "The Contemporary Theory of Metaphor." In *Metaphor and Thought,* 2nd ed., edited by Andrew Ortony, 202–51. Cambridge University Press.

Lakoff, George, and Mark Johnson. 2003/1980. *Metaphors We Live By.* University of Chicago Press.

Lancet, The. 2020. "COVID-19 in the USA: A Question of Time." *The Lancet* 395(10232): P1229. https://www.thelancet.com/journals/lancet/article/PIIS0140-6736(20)30863-1/fulltext.

Limbaugh, Rush. 2018. "This Invasion Is Erasing the American Culture. Where's the Wall?" *Rush Limbaugh Show,* November 29. https://www.rushlimbaugh.com/daily/2018/11/29/this-invasion-is-erasing-the-american-culture-wheres-the-wall/.

Lincoln, Yvonna S., and Egon G. Guba. 1985. *Naturalistic Inquiry.* Newbury Park, CA: SAGE.

Linde, Charlotte. 2000. "The Acquisition of a Speaker by a Story: How History Becomes Memory and Identity." *Ethos* 28(4): 608–32.

Little, Jack. 2016. "Children in Images: A Legal and Discursive Reframing of Child Sexual Abusive Imagery Online." College scholars senior project, University of Tennessee.

Lopez, German. 2016. "The Sneaky Language Today's Politicians Use to Get Away with Racism and Sexism." *Vox,* February 1. https://www.vox.com/2016/2/1/10889138/coded-language-thug-bossy.

Lorde, Audre. 1997. "A Litany for Survival." In *The Collected Poems of Audre Lorde.* New York: W. W. Norton.

Loseke, Donileen R. 2007. *Thinking about Social Problems: An Introduction to Constructionist Perspectives,* 2nd ed. New Brunswick, NJ: Transaction.

Luke, Allan. 2002. "Beyond Science and Ideology Critique: Developments in Critical Discourse Analysis." *Annual Review of Applied Linguistics* 22: 96–110.

Lynas, Mark. 2020. "COVID: Top 10 Current Conspiracy Theories." Cornell Alliance For Science, April 20. https://allianceforscience.cornell.edu/blog/2020/04/covid-top-10-current-conspiracy-theories/.

Machin, David, and Andrea Mayr. 2012. *How to Do Critical Discourse Analysis.* Los Angeles: SAGE.

Mäkelä, Maria. 2018. "Lessons from the Dangers of Narrative Project: Toward a Story-Critical Narratology." *Tekstualia* 1(4): 175–86.

Marcus, David. 2019. "Today Hundreds of Migrants Stormed the Border. What Do We Do When It's Thousands?" *The Federalist,* November 25. https://thefederalist.com/2018/11/25/today-hundreds-migrants-stormed-border-thousands/.

Manji, Rahim, Lois Presser, and Leigh T. Dickey. 2014. "Passivity, Harm, and Injustice." *Contemporary Justice Review* 17(1): 47–62.

Martin, Jennifer. 2015. "Conceptualizing the Harms Done to Children Made the Subjects of Sexual Abuse Images Online." *Child & Youth Services* 36(4): 267–87.

Martin, Jonathan, and Amie Parnes. 2008. "McCain: Obama Not an Arab, Crowd Boos." *Politico,* October 10. https://www.politico.com/story/2008/10/mccain-obama-not-an-arab-crowd-boos-014479

Matsuoka, Atsuko, and John Sorenson. 2001. *Ghosts and Shadows: Construction of Identity and Community in an African Diaspora.* University of Toronto Press.

Mauer, Marc. 2006. *Race to Incarcerate,* 2nd ed. New York: New Press.

McIntosh, Janet. 2020. "How Does Trump Use Coded Speech to Speak to His Base?" *BrandeisNOW,* October 2020. https://www.brandeis.edu /now/2020/october/election-trump-code-mcintosh.html.

McKinley, Jesse, and Luis Ferré-Sadurní. 2021. "With State in Crisis, Cuomo Outlines Plan to 'Win the Covid War'." *New York Times,* January 11. https://www.nytimes.com/2021/01/11/nyregion/cuomo-state-coronavirus-budget.html.

Messner, Steven F., and Richard Rosenfeld. 2012. *Crime and the American Dream,* 5th ed. Belmont, CA: Wadsworth.

Migration Data Portal. 2021. "Migrant Deaths and Disappearances (May 7)." https://migrationdataportal.org/themes/migrant-deaths-and-disappearances.

Mills, C. Wright. 1959. *The Sociological Imagination.* Oxford University Press.

Mills, Charles W. 2007. "White Ignorance." In *Race and Epistemologies of Ignorance,* edited by Shannon Sullivan and Nancy Tuana, 13–38. State University of New York Press.

———. 2015. "Global White Ignorance." In *Routledge International Handbook of Ignorance Studies,* edited by Matthias Gross and Linsey McGoey, 217–27. London: Routledge.

Morefield, Scott. 2019. "Hannity Presses Nikki Haley on Whether Asking Ukrainians to Investigate Bidens Was 'Good Practice'." *Daily Caller,* November 11. https://dailycaller.com/2019/11/11/sean-hannity-nikki-haley-ukraine/.

Murray, Amy Jo, and Kevin Durrheim, eds. 2019a. *Qualitative Studies of Silence: The Unsaid as Social Action.* Cambridge University Press.

Murray, Amy Jo, and Kevin Durrheim. 2019b. "Introduction: A Turn to Silence." In *Qualitative Studies of Silence: The Unsaid as Social Action,* edited by Amy Jo Murray and Kevin Durrheim, 1–20. Cambridge University Press.

Namaste, Viviane. 2000. *Invisible Lives: The Erasure of Transsexual and Transgendered People.* University of Chicago Press.

Narayan, Bhuva, Donald O. Case, and Sylvia L. Edwards. 2011. "The Role of Information Avoidance in Everyday-Life Information Behaviors." *Proceedings of the 74th ASIS&T (American Society for Information Science and Technology) Annual Meeting,* New Orleans, October 9–13.

National Right to Life. n.d. "Key Abortion Legislation." https://cqrcengage .com/nrlc/legislation?4.

NBCConnecticut.com. 2020. "Full Transcript: NY Gov. Cuomo's Rallying Cry to 'Kick Coronavirus Ass'." *NBCConnecticut,* March 27. https://www.nbcconnecticut.com/news/coronavirus/full-transcript-ny-gov-cuomos-rallying-cry-to-kick-coronavirus-ass/2246237/.

New York Times. 2020. "Read the Letter from President Trump to America's Governors," March 26. https://www.nytimes.com/2020/03/26/us/trump-letter-to-governors-coronavirus.html.

Nietzsche, Friedrich. 1983. "On the Uses and Disadvantages of History for Life." In *Untimely Meditations,* edited by Daniel Breazeale and translated by R. J. Hollingdale, 57–123. Cambridge University Press.

Ningard, Holly. 2018. *Attorney Stories of Environmental Crime: Egregious Harms, Ideal Cases.* Unpublished dissertation, University of Tennessee.

Nixon, Richard M. 1968. "Richard M. Nixon Presidential Nomination Acceptance Speech," August 8. http://www.4president.org/speeches/nixon1968acceptance.htm.

Norrick, Neal R. 1997. "Twice-Told Tales: Collaborative Narration of Familiar Stories." *Language in Society* 26(2): 199–220.

———. 2005. "The Dark Side of Tellability." *Narrative Inquiry* 15(2): 323–43.

———. 2012. "Remembering for Narration and Autobiographical Memory." *Language and Dialogue* 1(2): 193–215.

Nossel, Suzanne. 2021. "Opinion: Don't Let Trump's Second Trial Change the First Amendment." *New York Times,* January 14. https://www.nytimes.com/2021/01/14/opinion/trump-trial-incitement.html.

Offit, Anna. 2019. "Storied Justice: The Narrative Strategies of U.S. Federal Prosecutors." In *The Emerald Handbook of Narrative Criminology,* edited by Jennifer Fleetwood, Lois Presser, Sveinung Sandberg, and Thomas Ugelvik, 45–62. Bingley, UK: Emerald.

Olson, Tyler. 2020. "Trump Worries US Will See 'Suicides by the Thousands' If Coronavirus Devastates Economy." Fox News, March 25. https://www.foxnews.com/politics/trump-says-u-s-will-have-suicides-by-the-thousands-if-economic-slowdown-lasts-too-long.

Opotow, Susan. 1993. "Animals and the Scope of Justice." *Journal of Social Issues* 49(1): 71–85.

Opotow, Susan, Emese Ilyes, and Michelle Fine. 2019. "Silence in the Court: Moral Exclusion at the Intersection of Disability, Race, Sexuality, and Methodology." In *Qualitative Studies of Silence: The Unsaid as*

Social Action, edited by Amy Jo Murray and Kevin Durrheim, 107–25. Cambridge University Press.

Oprysko, Caitlin. 2020. "Trump Drafts Everyday Americans to Adopt His Battlefield Rhetoric." *Politico,* May 9. https://www.politico.com/news/2020/05/09/donald-trump-coronavirus-wartime-rhetoric-245566.

O'Reilly, Bill. 2019. Twitter, August 13. https://twitter.com/BillOReilly/status/1161246021650804737.

Orwell, George. 1968. "Politics and the English Language." In *The Collected Essays, Journalism and Letters of George Orwell,* Vol. 4: *In Front of Your Nose, 1945–1950,* edited by Sonia Orwell and Ian Angus, 127–40. New York: Harcourt, Brace, Jovanovich.

Otto, Natália. 2020. "'I Did What I Had to Do': Loyalty and Sacrifice in Girls' Narratives of Homicide in Southern Brazil." *British Journal of Criminology* 60: 703–21.

Partington, Alan. 2018. "Intimations of 'Spring'? What Got Said and What Didn't Get Said about the Start of the Middle Eastern/North African Uprisings: A Corpus-Assisted Discourse Study of a Historical Event." In *Exploring Silence and Absence in Discourse: Empirical Approaches,* edited by Melani Schröter and Charlotte Taylor, 95–123. Cham, Switzerland: Palgrave Macmillan.

Peters, Jeremy W., Michael M. Grynbaum, Keith Collins, Rich Harris, and Rumsey Taylor. 2019. "The New Nativists: How the El Paso Killer Echoed the Incendiary Words of Conservative Media Stars." *New York Times,* August 11. https://www.nytimes.com/interactive/2019/08/11/business/media/el-paso-killer-conservative-media.html.

Petintseva, Olga. 2019. "Reflections after 'Socrates Light': Eliciting and Countering Narratives of Youth Justice Officials." In *The Emerald Handbook of Narrative Criminology,* edited by Jennifer Fleetwood, Lois Presser, Sveinung Sandberg, and Thomas Ugelvik, 87–108. Bingley, UK: Emerald.

Phelan, James. 1989. *Reading People, Reading Plots: Character, Progression, and the Interpretation of Narrative.* University of Chicago Press.

———. 2008. "Narratives in Contest; or, Another Twist in the Narrative Turn." *PMLA* 123(1): 166–75.

———. 2017. *Somebody Telling Somebody Else: A Rhetorical Poetics of Narrative.* Ohio State University Press.

Plummer, Ken. 2019. *Narrative Power: The Struggle for Human Value.* Cambridge: Polity.

Polanyi, Livia. 1989. *Telling the American Story: A Structural and Cultural Analysis of Conversational Storytelling.* MIT Press.

Politico. 2020. "Andrew Cuomo Responds to Trump Calling Him a Strong Democratic Opponent to Biden." *Politico,* March 31. https://www.politico.com/video/2020/03/30/andrew-cuomo-responds-to-trump-calling-him-a-strong-democratic-opponent-to-biden-070371.

Polletta, Francesca. 2006. *It Was Like a Fever: Storytelling in Protest and Politics.* University of Chicago Press.

———. 2009. "How to Tell a New Story about Battering." *Violence against Women* 15(12): 1490–1508.

Polyzou, Alexandra. 2015. "Presupposition in Discourse: Theoretical and Methodological Issues." *Critical Discourse Studies* 12(2): 123–38.

Potter, Jonathan, and Margaret Wetherell. 1987. *Discourse and Social Psychology: Beyond Attitudes and Behaviour.* London: SAGE.

Presser, Lois. 2004. "Violent Offenders, Moral Selves: Constructing Identities and Accounts in the Research Interview." *Social Problems* 51(1): 82–101.

———. 2005. "Negotiating Power and Narrative in Research: Implications for Feminist Methodology." *Signs* 30(4): 2067–90.

———. 2008. *Been a Heavy Life: Stories of Violent Men.* University of Illinois Press.

———. 2009. "The Narratives of Offenders." *Theoretical Criminology* 13(2): 177–200.

———. 2012. "Getting on Top through Mass Murder: Narrative, Metaphor, and Violence." *Crime, Media, Culture* 8(1): 3–21.

———. 2013. *Why We Harm.* Rutgers University Press.

———. 2016. "Criminology and the Narrative Turn." *Crime, Media, Culture* 12(2): 137–51.

———. 2018. *Inside Story: How Narratives Drive Mass Harm.* University of California Press.

———. 2019. "The Story of Antisociality: Determining What Goes Unsaid in Dominant Narratives." In *The Emerald Handbook of Narrative Criminology,* edited by Jennifer Fleetwood, Lois Presser, Sveinung Sandberg, and Thomas Ugelvik, 409–24. Bingley, UK: Emerald.

Presser, Lois, and Suzanne Kurth. 2009. "'I Got a Quick Tongue': Negotiating Ex-convict Identity in Mixed Company." In *How Offenders Transform Their Lives,* edited by Bonita Veysey, Johnna Christian, and Damian J. Martinez, 72–86. Devon, UK: Willan.

Presser, Lois, and Sveinung Sandberg. 2015. "Introduction: What is the Story?" In *Narrative Criminology: Understanding Stories of Crime,* edited by Lois Presser and Sveinung Sandberg, 1–20. New York University Press.

Presser, Lois, Jennifer L. Schally, and Christine Vossler. 2020. "Life as a Reflexive Project: The Logics of Ethical Veganism and Meat-Eating." *Society & Animals* 28: 713–32.

Prince, Gerald. 1982. *Narratology: The Form and Functioning of Narrative.* Berlin: Walter de Gruyter.

———. 1988. "The Disnarrated." *Style* 22(1): 1–8.

———. 2003. *A Dictionary of Narratology,* rev. ed. University of Nebraska Press.

Radden, Günter, and Zoltán Kövecses. 1999. "Towards a Theory of Metonymy." In *Metonymy in Language and Thought,* edited by Klaus-Uwe Panther and Günter Radden, 17–59. Amsterdam: John Benjamins.

Re, Gregg. 2019. "No Mention of Bidens, Burisma while Ukraine Military Aid Was Held Up, State Official Testifies." Fox News, November 18. https://www.foxnews.com/politics/impeachment-bidens-burisma-ukraine-military-aid-state-official-testifies.

Reuters. 2020. "Amid Worsening Pandemic, Trump Pushes to Re-open U.S. for Business by Easter," March 24. https://www.reuters.com/article/us-health-coronavirus-usa-trump/amid-worsening-pandemic-trump-pushes-to-re-open-u-s-for-business-by-easter-idUSKB-N21B298.

Rice, Jenny. 2020. *Awful Archives: Conspiracy Theory, Rhetoric, and Acts of Evidence.* Ohio State University Press.

Ricoeur, Paul. 1991. "Life in Quest of Narrative." In *On Paul Ricoeur: Narrative and Interpretation,* edited by David Wood, 20–33. London: Routledge.

Riessman, Catherine Kohler. 2008. *Narrative Methods for the Human Sciences.* Thousand Oaks, CA: SAGE.

Ritchie, Hannah, Edouard Mathieu, Lucas Rodés-Guirao, Cameron Appel, Charlie Giattino, Esteban Ortiz-Ospina, Joe Hasell, Bobbie Macdonald, Diana Beltekian, and Max Roser. 2020. *Coronavirus Pandemic (COVID-19).* https://ourworldindata.org/coronavirus.

Romano, Andrew. 2008. "Red, White and Boo." *Newsweek,* October 11. https://www.newsweek.com/red-white-and-boo-219440.

Rosenblatt, Louise M. 1978. *The Reader, the Text, the Poem.* Southern Illinois University Press.

Russell, Aidan, ed. 2019. *Truth, Silence and Violence in Emerging States: Histories of the Unspoken.* Abingdon, Oxon: Routledge.

Russo, Carla Herreria. 2018. "The Real Story behind John McCain's Famous Campaign Rally Moment." *HuffPost,* August 26. https://www .huffpost.com/entry/mccain-defends-obama-real-story_n_5b821dffe4 b03485860129c4.

Sacks, Harvey. 1989. "Lecture Two: On Suicide Threats Getting Laughed Off." *Human Studies* 12 (3/4): 235–45.

Sacks, Harvey, Emanuel A. Schegloff, and Gail Jefferson. 1978. "A Simplest Systematics for the Organization of Turn Taking for Conversation." In *Studies in the Organization of Conversational Interaction,* edited by Jim N. Schenkein, 7–55. New York: Academic Press.

Sandberg, Sveinung. 2013. "Are Self-Narratives Strategic or Determined, Unified or Fragmented? Reading Breivik's Manifesto in Light of Narrative Criminology." *Acta Sociologica* 56 (1): 69–83.

———. 2016. "The Importance of Stories Untold: Life-Story, Event-Story, and Trope." *Crime, Media, Culture* 12: 153–71.

Sandberg, Sveinung, and Jan C. Andersen. 2019. "Opposing Violent Extremism through Counternarratives: Four Forms of Narrative Resistance." In *The Emerald Handbook of Narrative Criminology,* edited by Jennifer Fleetwood, Lois Presser, Sveinung Sandberg, and Thomas Ugelvik, 445–66. Bingley, UK: Emerald.

Sandberg, Sveinung, Sébastien Tutenges, and Heith Copes. 2015. "Stories of Violence: A Narrative Criminological Study of Ambiguity." *British Journal of Criminology* 55(6): 1168–86.

Savelsberg, Joachim. 2020. "Writing Biography in the Face of Cultural Trauma: Nazi Descent and the Management of Spoiled Identities." *American Journal of Cultural Sociology,* https://doi.org/10.1057 /s41290-020-00125-8.

———. 2021. *Knowing about Genocide: Armenian Suffering and Epistemic Struggles.* University of California Press.

Schally, Jennifer L. 2018. *Legitimizing Corporate Harm: The Discourse of Contemporary Agribusiness.* Cham, Switzerland: Palgrave Macmillan.

Schröter, Melani. 2019. "The Language Ideology of Silence and Silencing in Public Discourse: Claims to Silencing as Metadiscursive Moves in German Anti-Political Correctness Discourse." In *Qualitative Studies of Silence: The Unsaid as Social Action,* edited by Amy Jo Murray and Kevin Durrheim, 165–85. Cambridge University Press.

Schröter, Melani, and Charlotte Taylor, eds. 2018. *Exploring Silence and Absence in Discourse: Empirical Approaches.* Cham, Switzerland: Palgrave Macmillan.

Schwartzmann, Roy. 2015. "Sutured Identities in Jewish Holocaust Survivor Testimonies." *Journal of Social Issues* 71(2): 279–93.

Searle, John R. 1969. *Speech Acts: An Essay in the Philosophy of Language.* Cambridge University Press.

Shapiro, Jeffrey Scott. 2021. "No, Trump Isn't Guilty of Incitement." *Wall Street Journal,* January 10. https://www.wsj.com/articles/no-trump-isnt-guilty-of-incitement-11610303966.

Sharpe, Christina. 2016. *In the Wake: On Blackness and Being.* Duke University Press.

Sheriff, Robin E. 2000. "Exposing Silence as Cultural Censorship: A Brazilian Case." *American Anthropologist* 102: 114–32.

Singer, Peter. 1990. *Animal Liberation,* 2nd ed. New York: New York Review.

Simmel, Georg. 1906. "The Sociology of Secrecy and of Secret Societies." *American Journal of Sociology* 11(4): 441–98.

Sinnreich, Helene. 2008. "'And It Was Something We Didn't Talk About': Rape of Jewish Women during the Holocaust." *Holocaust Studies: A Journal of Culture and History* 14(2): 1–22.

Smith, Barbara Herrnstein. 1981. "Narrative Versions, Narrative Theories." In *American Criticism in the Post-Structuralist Age,* edited by Ira Konigsberg, 162–86. Ann Arbor: Michigan Studies in the Humanities.

Smith, Ben. 2008. "Muslims Barred from Picture at Obama Event." *Politico,* June 18. https://www.politico.com/story/2008/06/muslims-barred-from-picture-at-obama-event-011168.

Smith, David. 2019. "'Enemy of the People': Trump's War on the Media is a Page from Nixon's Playbook." *The Guardian,* September 7. https://www.theguardian.com/us-news/2019/sep/07/donald-trump-war-on-the-media-oppo-research.

Smith, Murray. 1995. *Engaging Characters: Fiction, Emotion, and the Cinema.* Oxford University Press.

Smith, Philip. 2005. Why War? The Cultural Logic of Iraq, the Gulf War, and Suez. University of Chicago Press.

Solórzano, Daniel G., and Tara J. Yosso. 2002. "Critical Race Methodology: Counter-Storytelling as an Analytical Framework for Education Research." *Qualitative Inquiry* 8(1): 23–44.

Spivak, Gayatri Chakravorty. 1988. "Can the Subaltern Speak?" In *Marxism and the Interpretation of Culture*, edited by Cary Nelson and Lawrence Grossberg, 271–313. Indiana University Press.

Sprunt, Barbara. 2020. "The History behind 'When the Looting Starts, the Shooting Starts'." National Public Radio, May 29. https://www.npr .org/2020/05/29/864818368/the-history-behind-when-the-looting-starts-the-shooting-starts.

Stannard, David E. 1992. *American Holocaust: The Conquest of the New World*. Oxford University Press.

Statista.com. 2021. "Number of Cumulative Cases of Coronavirus (COVID-19) in the United States from January 20, 2020 to March 3, 2021." Statista, March 4. https://www.statista.com/statistics/1103185 /cumulative-coronavirus-covid19-cases-number-us-by-day/.

Stibbe, Arran. 2001. "Language, Power and the Social Construction of Animals." *Society & Animals* 9: 145–61.

———. 2004. "Health and the Social Construction of Masculinity in *Men's Health* Magazine." *Men & Masculinities* 7(1): 31–51.

———. 2015. *Ecolinguistics: Language, Ecology and the Stories We Live By*. Abingdon, Oxon: Routledge.

Stockholder, Kay. 1998. "Lacan versus Freud: Subverting the Enlightenment." *American Imago* 55(3): 361–422.

Storrow, Richard F. 2013. "The Erasure of Egg Providers in Stem Cell Science." *Frontiers: A Journal of Women Studies* 34(3): 189–212.

Strand, Cecilia. 2018. "Cross-Media Studies as a Method to Uncover Patterns of Silence and Linguistic Discrimination of Sexual Minorities in Ugandan Print Media." In *Exploring Silence and Absence in Discourse: Empirical Approaches*, edited by Melani Schröter and Charlotte Taylor, 125–57. Cham, Switzerland: Palgrave Macmillan.

Strauss, Alix. 2020. "How a Home Health Aide Spends Her Sundays." *New York Times*, December 4. https://www.nytimes.com/2020/12/04 /nyregion/coronavirus-nyc-home-health-aide.html.

Strawson, Galen. 2004. "Against Narrativity." *Ratio* 17: 428–52.

Sue, Christina, and Mary Robertson. 2019. "Social Silences: Conducting Ethnographic Research on Racism in the Americas." In *Qualitative Studies of Silence: The Unsaid as Social Action*, edited by Amy Jo Murray and Kevin Durrheim, 71–88. Cambridge University Press.

Sue, Derald Wing. 2010. *Microaggressions in Everyday Life: Race, Gender, and Sexual Orientation*. Hoboken, NJ: John Wiley & Sons.

Swann, William B., Jr., Russell E. Johnson, and Jennifer K. Bosson. 2009. "Identity Negotiation at Work." *Research in Organizational Behavior* 29: 81–109.

Sykes, Gresham M., and David Matza. 1957. "Techniques of Neutralization." *American Sociological Review* 22(6): 664–70.

Tannen, Deborah. 1985. "Silence: Anything But." In *Perspectives on Silence,* edited by Deborah Tannen and Muriel Saville-Troike, 93–111. Norwood, NJ: Ablex.

Tannen, Deborah, and Muriel Saville-Troike. 1985. *Perspectives on Silence.* Norwood, NJ: Ablex.

Tennessee Department of Correction. n.d. "Tennessee Crime Victims' Bill of Rights." https://www.tn.gov/correction/redirect-agency-services /redirect-victim-services/tennessee-crime-victims--bill-of-rights.html.

Teo, Peter. 2000. "Racism in the News: A Critical Discourse Analysis of News Reporting in Two Australian Newspapers." *Discourse & Society* 11(1): 7–49.

Thomas, Jenny. 1995. *Meaning in Interaction: An Introduction to Pragmatics.* London: Longman.

Thomas, Katie. 2019. "Anti-Ageing Beauty Products: The Ones Your Bathroom Cabinet (and Face) Actually Need." *Marie Claire,* August 13. https://www.marieclaire.co.uk/beauty/skincare/anti-ageing-beauty-products-218183.

Titscher, Stefan, Michael Meyer, Ruth Wodak, and Eva Vetter. 2012. *Methods of Text and Discourse Analysis.* London: SAGE.

Toerien, Merran, and Clare Jackson. 2019. "Seeing Silenced Agendas in Medical Interaction: A Conversation Analytic Case Study." In *Qualitative Studies of Silence: The Unsaid as Social Action,* edited by Amy Jo Murray and Kevin Durrheim, 38–58. Cambridge University Press.

Travis, Jeremy, Bruce Western, and F. Stevens Redburn, eds. 2014. *The Growth of Incarceration in the United States: Exploring Causes and Consequences.* Washington, DC: National Academies Press.

Tuana, Nancy. 2006. "The Speculum of Ignorance: The Women's Health Movement and Epistemologies of Ignorance." *Hypatia* 21(3): 1–19.

Turley, Jonathan. 2021. "Swift New Impeachment Would Damage the Constitution." *The Hill,* January 11. https://thehill.com/opinion /judiciary/533469-swift-second-impeachment-would-damage-the-constitution.

Tutenges, Sébastien, and Sveinung Sandberg. 2013. "Intoxicating Stories: The Characteristics, Contexts and Implications of Drinking Stories among Danish Youth." *International Journal of Drug Policy* 24(6): 538–44.

UNICEF. 2017. "A Familiar Face: Violence in the Lives of Children and Adolescents." https://resourcecentre.savethechildren.net/pdf /violence_in_the_lives_of_children_and_adolescents.pdf/.

United States Sentencing Commission. 2020. "Crime Victims' Rights." https://www.ussc.gov/sites/default/files/pdf/training/primers/2020_ Primer_Crime_Victims.pdf.

van Dijk, Teun A. 1993. "Principles of Critical Discourse Analysis." *Discourse & Society* 4(2): 249–83.

———. 2014. *Discourse and Knowledge: A Sociocognitive Approach.* Cambridge University Press.

———. 2018. "Discourse and Migration." In *Qualitative Research in European Migration Studies,* edited by Ricard Zapata-Barrero and Evren Yalaz, 227–45. Cham, Switzerland: Springer.

van Hulst, Merlijn. 2019. "Ethnography and Narrative." *Policing and Society* 30(1): 98–115.

Van Leeuwen, Theo. 1995. "Representing Social Action." *Discourse & Society* 6(1): 81–106.

Van Voorhis, Patricia, and Lois Presser. 2003. "Women Offenders and Prison Classification: A Paradox." *Women, Girls and Criminal Justice* 4(1): 1–2, 9–11.

Venkataraman, Nina. 2018. "What's Not in a Frame? Analysis of Media Representations of the Environmental Refugee." In *Exploring Silence and Absence in Discourse: Empirical Approaches,* edited by Melani Schröter and Charlotte Taylor, 241–79. Cham, Switzerland: Palgrave Macmillan.

Vincent, Mary. 2010. "Breaking the Silence? Memory and Oblivion since the Spanish Civil War." In *Shadows of War: A Social History of Silence in the Twentieth Century,* edited by Efrat Ben-Ze'ev, Ruth Ginio, and Jay Winter, 47–67. Cambridge University Press.

Vinitzky-Seroussi, Vered, and Chana Teeger. 2010. "Unpacking the Unspoken: Silence in Collective Memory and Forgetting." *Social Forces* 88(3): 1103–22.

von Münchow, Patricia. 2018. "Theoretical and Methodological Challenges in Identifying Meaningful Absences in Discourse." In *Exploring Silence and Absence in Discourse: Empirical Approaches,* edited by Melani Schröter and Charlotte Taylor, 215–40. Cham, Switzerland: Palgrave Macmillan.

Wacquant, Loïc. 2009. *Punishing the Poor: The Neoliberal Government of Social Insecurity.* Duke University Press.

Warhol, Robyn R. 2005. "Neonarrative; or, How to Render the Unnarratable in Realist Fiction and Contemporary Film." In *A Companion to Narrative Theory,* edited by James Phelan and Peter J. Rabinowitz, 220–31. Malden, MA: Blackwell.

Walker, Anne Graffam. 1985. "The Two Faces of Silence: The Effect of Witness Hesitancy on Lawyers' Impressions." In *Perspectives on Silence,* edited by Deborah Tannen and Muriel Saville-Troike, 55–75. Norwood, NJ: Ablex.

Walsh, Joe. 2021. "FBI Director Says Atlanta Shooting 'Does Not Appear' Racially Motivated." *Forbes,* March 18. https://www.forbes.com/sites/joewalsh/2021/03/18/fbi-director-says-atlanta-shooting-does-not-appear-racially-motivated/.

Watts, Richard J. 1997. "Silence and the Acquisition of Status in Verbal Interaction." In *Silence: Interdisciplinary Perspectives,* edited by Adam Jaworski, 87–115. Berlin: Mouton de Gruyter.

Waxman, Zoë. 2003. "Unheard Testimony, Untold Stories: The Representation of Women's Holocaust Experiences." *Women's History Review* 12(4): 661–77.

Websdale, Neil, and Jeff Ferrell. 1999. "Taking the Trouble: Concluding Remarks and Future Directions." In *Making Trouble: Cultural Constructions of Crime, Deviance, and Control,* edited by Jeff Ferrell and Neil Websdale, 349–64. Hawthorne, NY: Aldine de Gruyter.

Welz, Claudia. 2016. "Trauma, Memory, Testimony: Phenomenological, Psychological, and Ethical Perspectives." *Scripta Instituti Donneriani Aboensis* 27: 104–33.

Wetherell, Margaret. 2013. "Affect and Discourse—What's the Problem? From Affect as Excess to Affective/Discursive Practice." *Subjectivity* 6(4): 349–68.

White, Hayden. 1980. "The Value of Narrativity in the Representation of Reality." *Critical Inquiry* 7(1): 5–27.

———. 1987. *The Content of the Form: Narrative Discourse and Historical Representation.* Johns Hopkins University Press.

White House. 2019. "Memorandum of Telephone Conversation, July 25." https://www.whitehouse.gov/wp-content/uploads/2019/09/Unclassified09.2019.pdf.

Whitford, Andrew B., and Jeff Yates. 2003. "Policy Signals and Executive Governance: Presidential Rhetoric in the War on Drugs." *Journal of Politics* 65(4): 995–1012.

Wildman, Stephanie M., and Adrienne D. Davis. 1995. "Language and Silence: Making Systems of Privilege Visible." *Santa Clara Law Review* 35(3): 881–906.

Wilstein, Matt. 2019. "Trevor Noah Mocks 'Idiot' Trump for Releasing 'Damning' Ukraine Transcript." *Daily Beast,* September 26. https://www.thedailybeast.com/daily-shows-trevor-noah-mocks-idiot-trump-for-releasing-damning-ukraine-transcript.

Winter, Jay. 2010. "Thinking about Silence." In *Shadows of War: A Social History of Silence in the Twentieth Century,* edited by Efrat Ben-Ze'ev, Ruth Ginio, and Jay Winter, 3–31. Cambridge University Press.

Wolfe, Lauren. 2015. "Infographic: Rape in War, by the Numbers." Women's Media Center, January 9. http://www.womensmediacenter.com/women-under-siege/infographic-rape-in-war-by-the-numbers.

Woloch, Alex. 2003. *The One vs. the Many: Minor Characters and the Space of the Protagonist in the Novel.* Princeton University Press.

World Health Organization (WHO). 2018a. "Air Pollution," May 2. https://www.who.int/airpollution/data/en/.

———. 2018b. "Climate Change and Health," February 1. https://www.who.int/news-room/fact-sheets/detail/climate-change-and-health.

———. 2019. "Drinking-Water," June 14. https://www.who.int/news-room/fact-sheets/detail/drinking-water.

Young, Jock. 1987. "The Tasks Facing a Realist Criminology." *Contemporary Crises* 11: 337–56.

Zerubavel, Eviatar. 2006. *The Elephant in the Room: Silence and Denial in Everyday Life.* Oxford University Press.

———. 2019. "Listening to the Sound of Silence: Methodological Reflections on Studying the Unsaid." In *Qualitative Studies of Silence: The Unsaid as Social Action,* edited by Amy Jo Murray and Kevin Durrheim, 59–70. Cambridge University Press.

Zhang, Xiaoye, and Xianliang Dong. 2019. "The Archived Criminal: Mandatory Prisoner Autobiography in China." In *The Emerald Handbook of Narrative Criminology,* edited by Jennifer Fleetwood, Lois Presser, Sveinung Sandberg, and Thomas Ugelvik, 427–44. Bingley, UK: Emerald.

Index

Abbott, H. Porter, 30
abortion, 92
absences, 113–27; bright side of, 131; communication, 20–21, 36, 135, 150n11; contexts, 85, 122; conversation analysis, 116; critical discourse analysis, 23–24, 33; definition of, 145; events, actions, experiences, 85; Ferrell, Jeff, 16; figurative expression, 66; Freud, Sigmund, 18; gaps, 22; Goffman, Erving, 11; harm, viii, 15–16, 17, 98; hauntology, 18; injustice, 17; interlocutors, 116; intertextuality, 125–26; Lacan, Jacques, 18–19; linguistics, 18, 22, 151n12; metaphors, 68; methodologies for unsaid analysis, x, 129, 130–31; metonymy, 68; narratives, 33, 80; Partington, Alan, 48; persons, 24, 85, 86–88, 89; perspectives, 17, 85, 89; politics, 94–95; power, 9, 11, 17, 115–16, 123; pragmatics, 19, 151n12; presences, 131–32; rape, 105; repression v, 151n1; silences, 139; speech, 17; stories, 24, 26, 124; texts, 9–13, 15–16, 17–18, 21, 36, 85, 86–88, 89, 98, 151n1;

unsaid, viii, 9–13, 36; unsaid analysis, 17–18, 63–64, 129, 131, 150n11. *See also* social construction of absences
adaptability, 29
Adkisson, Jim David, 124, 125
advertisements, 55
Agazino, Biko, 12–13
ageism, 91–92, 135
AIDS, 16
Ain't I a Woman (hooks), 86, 87
Alcántara-Plá, Manuel, 46–47, 94–95
Alexander, Jeffrey, 133
Allen, Graham, 113–14
ambiguous direction, 37–38, 40, 42–46, 65, 116, 145
Andrews, Molly, 32
animals. *See* nonhuman animals
antisociality, 59, 60–61
Arabs, 119–20, 155nn4–5
Austin, J. L., 43
authoritarian regimes, 5

Balakian, Peter, 126
Baldwin, James, 7–8
Bamberg, Michael, 29

185

Founded in 1893,
UNIVERSITY OF CALIFORNIA PRESS
publishes bold, progressive books and journals
on topics in the arts, humanities, social sciences,
and natural sciences—with a focus on social
justice issues—that inspire thought and action
among readers worldwide.

The UC PRESS FOUNDATION
raises funds to uphold the press's vital role
as an independent, nonprofit publisher, and
receives philanthropic support from a wide
range of individuals and institutions—and from
committed readers like you. To learn more, visit
ucpress.edu/supportus.